A TASTE OF FREEDOM

A CULINARY JOURNEY WITH AMERICA'S REFUGEES

WRITING	Vincent Delgado
PHOTOGRAPHY AND DESIGN	Jeremy Herliczek
PHOTOGRAPHY	Becky Shink

the Global Workshop, LLC

Printed in Lansing, MI, U.S.A.

1st Edition 2004

ISBN 0-9743168-0-6

Library of Congress Control Number 2003109146

ACKNOWLEDGEMENTS

Many organizations and people were critical to the completion of *A Taste of Freedom*. Though it would be impossible to name them all in this space, we are deeply indebted to them for their generosity, ideas, patience and support.

Our loved ones supported us throughout the process, understanding the missed family gatherings and long days spent in a busy test kitchen. We are extremely grateful to our parents Barbara Delgado, Siegfried and Janet Herliczek, and James and Sharon Shink.

The Diocese of Lansing and Catholic Relief Services helped fund our research and printing using proceeds from Operation Rice Bowl collections. To find out more about CRS, which is dedicated to assisting the poor outside the country, call (800) 736-3467.

The International Rescue Committee, founded in 1933 at the request of Albert Einstein to provide relief, protection and resettlement services to refugees and victims of oppression or violent conflict, helped fund the production and marketing of this book. For more information, call (877) REFUGEE.

Refugee Services, a program of Catholic Social Services of Lansing/St. Vincent Home, Inc., was invaluable to this project. The agency introduced us to refugee families and supported us in our work. A portion of the proceeds from this book will support the agency's work with refugees. For more information, call (517) 484-1010.

Many professional colleagues had direct roles in completing this book. We thank the Michigan State University School of Journalism, including Howard Bossen and Jim Detjen. Darcy Greene's critiques and suggestions were invaluable. We also thank Gretchen Wasper with BRD Printing and Dan Sutkovs for his graphics advice.

For direct introductions to the refugee families in this book, we thank: Tahani Ali, Lesley Baribeau, Natheer Brifkani, Abdulaziz Osman, Anne Phuong Nguyen, Carola Ravelo, Xue Vue and Besim Zeka. Without their help, this book would not have been possible.

For their critiques of the recipes and initial copy, we thank: Barbara Delgado, Elise Desjardins, Janet Herliczek, Sean Santos, Sharon Shink, Susan Shink and Karen Wischer. Cathy Bacile edited the manuscript. We owe her for her time and knowledge. Without her command of the English language we would have been lost.

Finally, we thank the families of the women depicted in this book. They were deeply involved in its completion. Thank you for feeding us and telling us your stories.

"I believe in the sun even if it isn't shining.
I believe in love even when I am alone.
I believe in God even when He is silent."
AN UNKNOWN REFUGEE
WORLD WAR II

This book is dedicated to:

Isha Abdi
Remzija Ademi
Zohiris Aguilar Calleja
Maria Clara Jaramillo Velazquez
Suad Finde
Sara Musa
Manivanh Ratdavong
Wasima

For opening their homes and their hearts.

And to all refugees across the globe
known and unkown
for believing.

CONTENTS

INTRODUCTION

In 1998, I was a City Hall reporter in a small Midwestern city. My world was political contributions, campaigns and sewer projects. The pace was fast. The subject matter interesting. But emotional attachment was difficult. Objectivity is a given in a just-the-facts profession. Emotion is often something you try to ignore in journalism. Mid-sized newspapers can be unforgiving places. The emphasis is on production. The attitude is bravado and bluster.

One day, my editors assigned me the annual Thanksgiving piece. For them, it was a simple assignment. Cover someone in poverty. Get some inspirational quotes about giving thanks. Write the required hearts and flowers copy.

The family was from Bosnia. My job was to meet them at their apartment and hear their story. Write it up. Move on to the next piece. I was interested in the story, but didn't think much about it. There wasn't time for that. There was always the next story to write. And I'd seen these refugees, these immigrants, before. They clean our hotel rooms, sew our clothes, care for our aging parents. I'd seen refugees at bus stops and wandering the city's empty downtown. This would be a simple assignment.

It wasn't so simple.

The next two days revealed a new America, an America built by an underclass of heroes no one knows. It's an America of intense poverty, accented voices and calculated risks. It's an America of backbreaking first jobs in factories, sweaty kitchens and laundries, where the emphasis is on hard work, not on the ability to speak English. It is also an America of hope for these refugees, these former doctors, lawyers, activists, nurses, teachers and politicians. While they struggle with new lives and nightmares, their children become principals and cabinet members, optometrists and real estate tycoons. Most refugees eventually learn English, buy homes, pay taxes and return to their professions as American citizens.

They come to the United States under a process that can take as long as five years. They come with little choice. Their options are simple: Flee or be killed because of their political beliefs, religion, race, gender or nationality. They are here because they have to be—because they helped the U.S. in Vietnam, were born Croatian instead of Serbian, served as women leaders in Taliban Afghanistan or protested against using children as soldiers in Sudan. They are believers in a better world. They are believers in family, in love, in God, in democracy. And for that, many times, they must flee. They are not here to clean our hotel rooms, to sew our clothes or take care of our aging parents. They want to go home. But home is no option.

This is the America I walked into the day I met a family from Bosnia in a cramped apartment on downtown's western edge. This was a new world. A world of men with guns at night. Of running, always running. A world of war.

That first day I saw photographs and heard stories. I saw a beautiful home in the mountains destroyed by war. I saw a beauty salon burned to the ground. I heard of a mother's tears. I listened to sadness and survival. I heard of airports and documents and loss and despair and, ultimately, hope.

The second day, Thanksgiving, they fed me. It's what Thanksgiving is about, they told me, dismissing my journalistic protests of the need for objectivity. And over the years, I learned, it was never an issue of objectivity. The act of giving, of feeding, is what refugees are about. In every refugee home, since that day in a Bosnian living room, I have been given food. Curries from Afghanistan, marinated chicken from Cuba, soup from the Hmong hills of Laos, tea from Kurdistan. Every living room is a different country. Every food, a different story.

I didn't know it then, but that day in a Bosnian living room, eating Pite and roasted chicken and sipping homemade plum brandy—*A Taste of Freedom* was born. Part biography, part documentary, part cookbook, the pages that follow are an attempt to chronicle the lives of refugee women through one of the few things they could bring with them: their food.

Food is what defines us. Its aromas tell secrets in fire and steam. We relive history in the spices of home. Food is our culture, our belief, our memory.

It was always the food in these homes that brought out the memories. The stories we must never forget. Memories of making pastries with mothers in Kosovo. Of sitting with husbands for dinner in Sudan. Of teaching daughters to cook in Vietnam.

It is a fascinating world. These living rooms. These refugee kitchens.

They are the living rooms of our parents and grandparents, the kitchens of our mothers and grandmothers. Our ancestors looking for a New World on the Santa Maria, at Plymouth Rock, on Ellis Island. This was the America I had searched for in the boardrooms of City Hall and in the deadlines of journalism.

I quit my job and entered this new American world.

I went to work at a resettlement agency for refugees. Until the Bosnian story, I had never heard of these agencies. I didn't know that they are all over the country, resettling as many as 110,000 U.S. State Department–approved refugees into the inner cities of our nation. I didn't know that, without refugees, the population of my city would have dropped markedly or that my school district would have lost even more students. I learned that it was refugees who were bringing the rebirth of our cities' crumbling cores. It was refugees who brought vibrancy to our cities and valedictorians to our schools.

I learned that every one of these agencies is in need of help. With almost nothing in government funding, they rely on donations to fill refugee homes with furniture, compassionate landlords to accept tenants with no credit, business owners to employ people with no English skills, and volunteers to teach English and become their friends.

The more I learned, the more I was shocked that nobody knew anything about this refugee America. The media—the world I came from—confused refugees and immigrants and undocumented aliens on a daily basis. To them, refugees are simply foreigners. The ones that clean our hotel rooms, sew our cloths and care for our parents. There is no need for memories. No need for food.

And in this mediated ignorance, Sept. 11, 2001, hit. None of the terrorists were refugees. None entered through the U.S. Refugee Resettlement Program. But refugees—as foreigners—suddenly were suspect. Newspapers covered refugee issues as part of the war on terror. States began to make it hard for refugees to get identification, despite legal immigration documents and approvals from the United Nations, the U.S. State Department and the U.S. Justice Department. Seeking votes, politicians began adding more hurdles for refugees to come to the United States. Refugee annual admissions were halved, then halved again and then reduced to almost nothing in 2003. Suddenly refugees, these heroes, many of whom were in jeopardy because they helped the U.S. in wars for democracy, wars on terror, were a dangerous group. They were not to be trusted.

I was not alone in the discovery of this new America. Jeremy Herliczek, a photojournalist and a good friend, and Becky Shink, a photojournalist and my wife, heard my tales of refugees. Soon, they joined me for tea in living rooms across the city. Jeremy spent time working at the refugee agency and researched refugees for his masters program while Becky and I became foster parents of two refugee teens from Sudan. The work was infectious. Every refugee we met had a new story and a new food to try. They opened their lives to us.

We learned that these were not the homes of the "dangerous" foreigners portrayed on the nightly news. We didn't need increasing crackdowns on our civil liberties to protect ourselves from these heroes. These believers. These "huddled masses yearning to breathe free," in the poet Emma Lazarus' words. Theirs are the stories of America, itself. As liberty's door creaked shut in America, refugees needed the golden lamp of understanding, not repression.

It was time for a book.

In these pages, you will find the stories of daughters, mothers and grandmothers from eight different countries. Some are finding new lives and new hope. Some are still living with nightmares. These women picked out the recipes, taught us how to prepare them and let us into their lives.

It is our sincere hope that the food and the stories will inspire you and your loved ones as much as they did us. We hope that through *A Taste of Freedom*, you will discover this new America and want to become a part of it. Indeed, you already are. A portion of the proceeds from this book will be donated for direct services to newly arrived refugees. But there is always more to do. Refugees need people like you. And your involvement is simply a phone call away. To help, check your phone directory under "Refugee" or "Community Organizations." At times, the names of the agencies conceal their work with refugees. So you may need to search the Internet under "Refugee" and the name of your town. Call the agency and ask what they need. Also the International Rescue Committee at www.theirc.org and the U.S. Committee for Refugees at www.refugees.org are good sources for more information on refugees. Get informed. Get involved. This new America awaits.

Vincent Delgado
The Global Workshop, LLC
August 6, 2003

KOSOVO

In 1998, nearly 1 million Kosovar Albanians fled Serb paramilitaries battling rebels for control of this Serbian province the size of Connecticut. Christian Orthodox Serbians see Kosovo as the cradle of their civilization. Ethnic Muslim Albanians believe they are descendents of a Balkan tribe from the area. In early 1999, NATO airstrikes ended widespread massacres, though thousands were killed before hostilities ceased. More than 14,000 Kosovars resettled in the U.S. and 25 percent have since returned to Kosovo. Today, the province is governed by the United Nations Interim Administration Mission, which is slowly relinquishing control.

Remzija Ademi can't stand the smell of tuna fish.

The smell in the cans of fish passed out day and night by the food people should stay where it belongs: In Macedonia's Stankovic II refugee camp.

And she hates the loamy smell of the earth in spring.

It should stay in the mud flowing under the big blue tarps of U.N. tents—beneath the spring rains that pour over what is left of the Balkans.

And she gags at the sweet, milky odor of cafeteria buffets.

The macaroni and cheese. The hot dogs. The empty, red and white pint cartons of milk piled high in industrial trash cans. They should remain ghosts wafting through the barracks of Fort Dix, New Jersey, in the summer of 1999.

♦   ♦   ♦

But Remzija, 32, remembers all of it. The rotten tuna fish. The filth. The sour milk.

It is the smell of war.

And she still can't stand it.

She can't stand even the thought of it. The smell. The odor.

And yet.

The war hasn't ended yet for Remzija, her husband Rabit and their children. It's still there.

There, in the scars lining the body of her executed brother-in-law on autopsy videos from Kosovo.

There, in the sudden announcement from her son Perparim, age nine: *Some people are bad. Some people cut other people's heads off and use them for soccer.*

There, in the family's unpaid utility bills and the lost jobs and the cramped apartment in south Lansing.

The war lingers like a dinner left half eaten.

Like hot dogs and macaroni and cheese in a barracks cafeteria.

And Remzija is shocked by it. This is not her life. This is not the way it was supposed to be.

It was supposed to be Kosovo in 1998.

♦   ♦   ♦

Kosovo, 1998.

Remzija lived with Rabit and her children in a big house in the small, mountain village of Vilkinca.

Vilkinca. A quiet place—one of the last small bits of the Old Country left in modern Europe. Remzija did chores with other women in the village. The men worked construction. The women and the men worked hard.

There were always lots of friends around, she recalls.

As was custom, Remzija had moved into Rabit's family home when the two married. But she thought often of her father—as she does today. How he would come home from the flour factory, scrubbed clean—not a speck of flour dusting his brow.

And that is what Remzija thinks of when she remembers Kosovo before.

Her aging father miles away.

The flour factory.

Her father—scrubbed clean.

♦   ♦   ♦

But in the spring of 1998, Remzija watched Kosovo crumble on the nightly news.

The call for a Muslim Kosovo separate from greater Serbia.

The U.N. decision to back independence. The midnight marches by Serbian police.

The refugees walking. Hundreds walking. Always walking.

By 1999, the war began showing up at Remzija's door in Vilkinca. Friends of friends. Distant relatives. Tired faces with news of darkness spreading across Kosovo. These refugees lived on the third floor of the family home.

Remzija remembers.

They said very little.

By April 1999, the Serbian police came to Vilkinca. There was no midnight knock. No bullhorn warning.

Nothing.

They simply crashed through the door. One moment it was there. The next it was shattered in splinters and glass.

All of it shattered.

In one instant.

The mountains. The Old Country village. The chores on the farm. The men building. The children playing.

All of it shattered into splinters and glass and men with black guns and painted faces.

And then Remzija was running. Grabbing crying children. Her husband's shocked face. Out the door. The house blurry through tears. Down the path. Into the street.

No time for possessions.

No time for recollection.

No time.

◆　　◆　　◆

Michigan, 2003.

It's snowing outside in the parking lot on the south side. The children are inside. They are loud and wild. It's been too cold to go out for days.

Inside, the house is warm. Remzija's face is flush. She wipes the sweat from her face. The newscaster on satellite Kosovo television rattles on about the winner of a beauty contest. Remzija laughs at the kids, wipes a lock of hair from her sweaty brow and bends down to rotate the Pite, the family's favorite dish, rising in a huge pan in the oven.

Her husband loves Pite. So do the kids. So does everyone from Kosovo.

When we eat Pite, we feel like we're back in Kosovo, her husband says.

Remzija bends to turn the Pite once again. Her face is flush. She is nearly nine months pregnant and the kids are wild.

It's too cold outside to play.

And the old house is gone.

There was no time.

Remzija stands, her hand on her back. She stretches.

She laughs and wipes a stray lock of hair from her brow. She sighs.

She whispers.

It all feels like forever.

Guests in Kosovar homes are treated to small glasses of pure Ceylon tea.

Kosovar
Culture & Cuisine

Food in Kosovo reflects the influence of its different occupiers over the centuries.

In ancient times the Balkans were held by the Greeks and the Romans. Kosovars still have Greek-inspired stuffed vegetables on the menu.

Next, the Ottoman Turks held the entire area for more than 500 years, bringing a Mediterranean and Middle Eastern influence. Today, Kosovars are fans of Dolma, stuffed grape leaves and Qofte, typical from Sudan to Afghanistan. Some say Pite, the signature of dish of the entire former Yugoslavia, is inspired by the meat and spinach pies still popular in Turkey.

In 1912, Serbs defeated the Ottoman Turks in the first Balkan War, bringing Slavic influences to the food, such as the Hungarian paprika found in Ariz Ma Mesh.

And finally, Soviet rule homogenized and lightened food throughout the Balkans, bringing crisp, Albanian Sheqerpare sugar cookies to Kosovo.

Many say a completely Kosovar cuisine is now developing in the newly independent Kosovo—as is occurring in the new republics of Croatia, Serbia and Montenegro.

But Remzija holds tight to the traditions from the rambling house in Vilkinca, cooking the Kosovar dishes she learned in her mother's kitchen at age 11.

As a refugee in a camp in Macedonia and Fort Dix, New Jersey, Remzija had one thing in mind:

I had to get an oven to cook bread.

She cooks bread every morning and lays out a Western-style spread of food every night. Pure Ceylon tea is always served.

It's what we do in Kosovo. It's what I do here, she said.

Sheqerpare
Cookies in Syrup

With desserts like these super-sweet, glazed sugar cookies and baklava common at Remzija's, it's clear that to be a Kosovar means to have a serious sweet tooth. Try these cookies and you will too. The cloves and vanilla give the cookies a particularly Kosovar taste. We adapted this recipe from Kosovars in the Lansing area and the cookbook "Albanian Cooking" by Klementina and R. John Hysa.

2 **cups sugar**

¾ **cup butter, softened**

2 **egg yolks**

2 **cups flour**

¼ **teaspoon baking soda**

½ **cup water**

6 **whole cloves**

¼ **teaspoon vanilla extract**

Preheat oven to 350°F.

Mix 1 cup of the sugar with the butter in a large mixing bowl. Add egg yolks and stir until the mixture is smooth. Then add the flour and baking soda and mix until a smooth, cookie dough forms.

Roll out the dough to about ⅛-inch thickness and cut into 2-inch rounds with a cookie cutter or the top of a glass. Place the rounds on greased baking sheets and bake for 10 to 15 minutes or until the cookies are pale gold and their edges are just beginning to turn brown. Remove and allow the cookies to cool on the baking sheets.

As the cookies bake, make the syrup by mixing the remaining cup of sugar, water and cloves in a one-quart saucepan. Bring the mixture to a boil under medium/high heat, stirring constantly. Boil until the syrup begins to thicken. This should take about 10 to 15 minutes.

Remove the mixture from the heat and add the vanilla. Pour the hot syrup over the cookies. Serve at room temperature.

Makes 48 cookies

Ariz Ma Mesh
Rice with Steak

This is a spicy main course with loads of paprika. Depending on the type of paprika used, the dish can be incredibly hot. You can find Dafinka Spice, a mix of salt, dried vegetables and spices, in some import stores. Made by Vitaminka in Macedonia, it is distributed by Tut's International Co. in Dearborn, Michigan. Call them at (313) 582-9100 to find it in your area.

1 cup uncooked rice
2 cups water
½ teaspoon salt
1 pound round steak, cut into one-inch cubes
1½ tablespoons Dafinka Spice
3 ounces sweet yellow onions (½ cup), diced
1 tablespoon vegetable oil
1 heaping tablespoon paprika

Preheat oven to 450°F.

Bring rice and water to a boil over high heat on a stovetop in a 14-inch round baking pan, 2 inches or deeper. Reduce to a simmer and cook for 45 minutes. Keep enough liquid in the rice to keep it the consistency of a thick broth. Add the salt 20 minutes into the process. Stir often.

Meanwhile, place the steak in a 2-quart saucepan with enough water to cover the meat. Simmer for 10 minutes. Drain the water and replace with enough fresh water to cover the meat. Simmer for an additional 10 minutes or until the meat is cooked all the way through. Add the broth from the beef and the Dafinka Spice to the simmering rice.

Fry the onions in the oil in a skillet until they become translucent, add the paprika and mix well. When the rice is ready, add the mixture, mix well and remove from heat. Carefully add the cooked meat to the center of the pan. Drizzle the rice broth over the meat to keep it moist.

Bake the rice and beef mixture in the oven for 10 minutes or until a slight crust develops on top. Cool 10 minutes and serve with Pite.

Serves 6 to 8

Pite
See recipe on the next page

Pite
Kosovar Stuffed Pastry **(SEE PHOTOGRAPH PREVIOUS PAGE)**

S ay the word Pite (pronounced pea-ta) to any Kosovar and eyes light up. It is the region's signature dish. Pite is to Kosovo what pizza is to Italy. This sixteen-layered Balkanized pastry can be filled with just about anything—Feta cheese, spinach, curried meat. Remzija's favorite filling is green onions and eggs. She says it's good with a little cottage cheese, too.

4 cups flour

2 tablespoons salt

2½ cups water

2 large eggs

3 bunches green onions, chopped

2 cups small curd cottage cheese

1 cup vegetable oil

Preheat oven to 500°F.

Mix the flour, ½ tablespoon of salt, and 2 cups water in a large plastic mixing bowl with a fork. Then knead with your hands. Add additional water or flour as necessary to form an elastic dough that does not readily stick to your hands. Cut the dough and form into 2 equal-sized balls. Dust the dough-balls with flour and cover with a clean dishtowel. Let stand for 15 minutes.

Meanwhile, mix the eggs, green onions, cottage cheese and remaining salt in a large mixing bowl and set aside.

Sprinkle a large work surface with flour. Pour a ½-cup of vegetable oil into a measuring cup and set aside.

Roll the first dough ball with a rolling pin into a 20-inch diameter circle, working carefully from the center outwards to ensure that the dough is as uniformly thin as possible. Moisten the flattened dough by spreading ¼-cup of oil across the entire 20-inch diameter of the circle. Stretch the rolled dough an additional 4 inches in diameter, being careful not to tear it.

Lay a 10-inch diameter plate in the center of the rolled dough and make 8 equal cuts with a butter knife from the edge of the plate to the edge of the circle. Remove the plate. The cuts should form eight equal-sized "petals" with a 10-inch diameter center remaining uncut. Fold the petals across the inside one at a time, carefully stretching out the sides and tucking them under the 10-inch center. Use your fingertips and a small amount of oil from the measuring cup to moisten each petal after it has been laid, stretched and tucked. Repeat this step until all the petals have been folded across the inside, stretched and tucked under and the remaining ¼ cup of oil has been used. The result should be a 10-inch circle of eight layers of dough about 1 inch in total thickness. Set aside.

Pour a second ½-cup of oil in the measuring cup, sprinkle additional flour across the work surface and repeat procedure with the second dough ball.

Roll out the first 10-inch, 8-layered circle of dough to the size of a pizza pan or about 18 inches in diameter. Spread the green onion, egg and cheese mixture across the dough and set aside.

Roll out the second 10-inch, eight-layered circle of dough to the same size as the first. Place on top of the first 18-inch crust, tuck the edges under and seal the seam well, using a small amount of water on your fingertips, if necessary.

Place the unbaked Pite onto a non-stick, 18-inch pizza pan and position in the center of the middle rack of the oven. Bake for 6 minutes, rotating occasionally.

Move the Pite to the oven's top rack and bake for an additional 6 minutes or until the Pite is nicely browned on top, rotating occasionally.

Remove from oven, splash the remaining water across the top of the Pite and then quickly cover with aluminum foil and towels. This will steam it for an additional 10 minutes.

Remove the aluminum foil and towel, cut into 8 slices and serve.

Serves 8

SOMALIA

One look at the CIA World Fact Book says it all about Somalia. Under the government subsection, the first word is "No." The country has no permanent government, no welfare state medical care, no national legal system, little food, small reserves of uncontaminated water and a severe lack of infrastructure of any kind. Instead, Somalia, a nation of civil war and factional fighting since 1991, is awash in weapons, land mines, lawlessness, kidnappings, hijackings and "technicals"—pickups mounted with high-caliber semi-automatic and automatic rifles. In 1992, at the height of the violence, 2 million Somalis became internally displaced and more than 800,000 fled Somalia—population 7.7 million. As of 2002, more than a half-million people had been killed, 400,000 were homeless and 300,000 remain abroad as refugees.

In conversation after conversation with refugees the same phrases crop up.

It was luck.

It was destiny, really.

The will of Allah.

God has given me more than I ever needed.

I am the luckiest woman alive.

Here are people who have lost everything, experienced unspeakable horrors and survived by their wits. But after all that, in their words, it is not they who made it. Not they who survived. No. In their words, their lives were *given to them. It was destiny. It was the will of Allah.*

Isha Abdi lost many things in the war in Somalia. She lost her home, her country, her mother and her health. And *it was a miracle.*

In fact, as we sit in her living room in a house that Habitat for Humanity built, it's clear that it was actually 13 miracles. Each of them greet us as we sip tea and talk. One is on her way to school. Another has brought Isha's grandchild for a visit. Another helps Isha prepare sambusas.

Her children survived Somalia, the chaos of camps in Kenya, a mother debilitated by stress. Four are in college, three in high school, three in middle school, one in elementary school and two are married.

It's because of them that I'm here. Their future is here in America, Isha says.

A refugee camp is no place for a child. In Kenya, where they lived for five years before coming to America, the average family lost three children.

All of Isha's children made it. A miracle.

◆   ◆   ◆

In 1990, death, not miracles, was all around Isha, her husband and their children. She felt it in the chilled silence of Mogadishu.

For weeks, there had been rumors of clan battles to come, of food being withheld in the ports, of guns and mortars and pickups stolen for a war that was to come. But, at that time, the city remained loud and boisterous. Business continued. Schools remained open. The streets were clogged as always. One day, Isha's husband, Abdulaziz, came home early from work as a manager of the Somali Savings and Commercial Bank. He ate lunch and took a nap out of the midday heat. Isha stayed up to clean, watch the younger children and prepare for the rest of the family's arrival home from school. It was Sunday, Dec. 3, 1990, a workday like any other in Somalia.

Then silence. The honking stopped. The shouts and laughter outside the family compound were gone. Mogadishu's cacophony had simply quit.

Isha woke her husband up.

Something is happening, she told him.

Abdulaziz left the house, telling Isha that if anyone came to attack their home, to give them anything the family had. He rushed to the children's school in the family's station wagon through a bizarre scene. No cars. Shuttered windows. Silence.

The city was empty, Abdulaziz remembers. *That was the beginning.*

Abdulaziz packed his children and the rest of the neighborhood children into the car and brought them home. Meanwhile, Isha peeked out a window.

I saw people running through the streets. Men with guns hijacking pickup trucks.

The bombing started at sundown. The technicals came out. The war had begun. The family fled for Merka, another part of the city that would be less dangerous. Abdulaziz' job was gone. The banks had been ransacked.

After a month, Merka became dangerous. They heard their neighborhood had calmed down. They returned to an empty house. Everything had been stolen. Food was scarce. One day as Isha walked through Mogadishu Stadium, the only safe route to a market rumored to have food, Isha saw five men lined up on the grass of the stadium. They were blindfolded.

I saw five men executed that day. That was my first time.

There would be more horror. One night, the war returned to their neighborhood. This time there was nowhere else to flee. Armed men climbed over the compound wall. They had heard Abdulaziz was a bank manager. Where was his gold, they demanded. The banks were empty. He must have it.

Abdulaziz had nothing to give them. He showed them an empty house.

They shot him nine times.

He was saved when Isha's mother jumped in front of the men. She died from her gunshot wounds. Abdulaziz still lives with two bullets that could not be removed.

The family lived in a hospital for nearly two months as Abdulaziz recovered. Then they fled to United Nations refugee camps in Kenya. But the nightmare continued.

War had followed fleeing Somalis to the camps. Clans fought there as they did in Mogadishu. Each night people were killed as they slept. Huts were burned. Children died from malnutrition. Everyone suffered from malaria.

Isha and her family lived there for five years.

◆   ◆   ◆

On March 27, 1997, they arrived in Lansing, more than six years after silence fell over Mogadishu. Isha held her daughter, Faduma, closely. She had been vomiting blood the entire trip. The family went straight to the hospital. Faduma was treated for an ulcer. Isha slept at her side.

They emerged from the hospital into silence.

A good kind of silence. The silence of the early morning. The silence of safe children and safe husbands. A miraculous silence.

When I saw that the city was quiet, she says, *I really liked it. It was good for my family. This was the best thing that ever happened to me.*

It was a miracle.

Isha often decorates her hands with henna tattoos, a custom popular throughout the region.

Somali
Culture & Cuisine

One look at a map of Somalia and two features stand out. First, the country makes a big right turn along the horn of Africa with a coastline stretching from Djibouti to the north and Kenya to the south. And, second, Somalia sits at sea level just 10 degrees north of the equator and temperatures routinely break 100°F.

Those two features, the coast and the sizzling heat, created a culture of incredible historical diversity that relies on family for survival.

The coastline has invited traders and mariners from across the world, bringing new ideas and foods for centuries. Since the 2nd century, Phoenicians, Persians, Greeks and Romans have landed on its shores in search of the region's legendary Frankincense and Myrrh. In the 10th century, Arab traders brought Islam and Indians brought Curry-Stuffed Turnovers eaten throughout the Muslim holiday of Ramadan.

Somalia's colonial period followed the opening of the Suez Canal in 1869 and the British and the Italians controlled the north and south of the country. The Italians brought pasta, known as baasto and crema caramella, known as Benadiri Cake. The Brits brought the concept of high tea, and the cardamom-laced tea, Shaah, became the national drink. So much so that Somalis regularly say: *A person who has not worked for something, tea is forbidden.* More loosely translated: *There is no free lunch.*

At the same time, the cruel heat makes reliance on a patriarchal family structure the only means of survival for most Somalis. Well over 50 percent are nomadic herders whose diet centers around meat and milk. The idea of a nation state was a foreign concept until the Europeans came. Some say it still is. Somalis don't ask *Where are you from?* They ask *Who are you from?*

Families are that important. Women mark important family events with henna tattoos on their hands and feet. Births are widely celebrated. Male births more so. Large families are rejoiced and extended families live in vast family compounds.

Shaah
Somali Tea

*S*omalis drink this strong, sweet tea in the morning, at the traditional British tea time of 4 p.m. and in the evening. The tea, spiced with cardamom, cinnamon, ginger and clove, is a version of chai tea sipped throughout the Middle East, North Africa and Central Asia. "Some people can't do without it," Isha says.

4 cups water

½ teaspoon cardamom seeds

1 3-inch cinnamon stick

½ teaspoon ground ginger

¼ cup sugar

1 teaspoon loose black tea (or 1 black tea bag)

Pulverize the ingredients in a mortar and pestle or coffee grinder until they are coarsely ground. Bring the ingredients to a boil in a teapot. Remove from heat and let steep about one minute. Pour through a strainer into tea cups.

Optional: Add some milk and/or a squirt of lime juice.

Serves 4

Sambusas
Curry-Stuffed Turnovers *(SEE PHOTOGRAPH ON PAGE 28)*

*C*runchy on the outside, spicy on the inside, Sambusas are the Somali equivalent of Indian Samosas. These stuffed and fried pastries are popular party foods throughout much of the world. You can find Sambusas in Ethiopia—served spritzed with lemon and stuffed with peppers and lentils. In Kajikstan, they are served with Chutney. Somali Sambusas are even served in Italy—a colonial occupier of Somalia for decades. They aren't as hard to make as they look. Keep the crust as thin as possible. Use patience and practice in folding the shells. Fry them well to make sure they are good and crispy. Isha says you can make them with chicken or even a nice mild fish.

2 medium potatoes, cut into ¼-inch cubes	Fry the potatoes in canola oil in a 9-inch skillet over medium heat until slightly firm. Remove from skillet and set aside.
1 tablespoon canola oil	
1 pound lean ground beef	

2 **medium potatoes,
cut into ¼-inch cubes**

1 **tablespoon canola oil**

1 **pound lean ground beef**

½ **pound sweet yellow
onions (1 cup), finely diced**

3½ **teaspoons salt**

5 **cloves garlic, finely
chopped**

1 **tablespoon curry**

½ **teaspoon pepper**

¼ **pound carrots (⅔ cup),
diced**

4¾ **cups flour**

1½ **cups water**

**vegetable oil for deep
frying**

Fry the potatoes in canola oil in a 9-inch skillet over medium heat until slightly firm. Remove from skillet and set aside.

Fry the ground beef in the same skillet with the onions and salt, over medium-high heat. As it fries, break apart the ground beef with a spoon and stir until nearly dry. Add the garlic, curry, pepper and 2 teaspoons of salt. Mix well and fry over medium heat until dry. Remove from heat, add potatoes and carrots and mix well.

Mix the flour, water and remaining salt until it forms a dough that is slightly elastic and does not stick to your hands. Add additional flour and water as necessary. Divide dough into 6 balls. Form into flat cakes of roughly 5 inches in diameter using a rolling pin. Keep the dough covered with a towel to protect it from drying out.

Take two cakes. Coat the top of the first with oil. Place the second on top and dust with flour. Roll the stack into a very flat crust about 14 to 16 inches in diameter. Cut the crust into 4 equal-sized triangles. Repeat until all the dough balls are used.

Place a triangle on a preheated skillet on medium high. When both sides are just slightly toasted, remove from heat and carefully peel apart into 2 very thin triangles. Repeat until all of the triangles have been peeled.

Mix enough flour and water in a bowl to make a "glue" for the shells. This mixture should have the consistancy of wood glue. Mix more as necessary.

Hold a triangle with rounded edge down. Fold and glue the lower corners over each other, forming a sealed cone, point down. As the cone is folded, the upper corner will create a flap on top.

Pack the cone with 2 heaping tablespoons of filling. Glue the upper flap down, creating a stuffed triangle. Repeat until all of the crust and filling is used.

Put 2 inches of oil in a deep 9-inch frying pan and heat over medium-high heat. Test with a couple of drops of water. When it sizzles strongly, add the turnovers and fry until they are a golden brown, turning often. Remove from oil, drain and cool.

Makes 24 Sambusas

Sambusas
See recipe previous page

Dolsho Benadiri
Benadiri Cake

D*espite its name, this thick custard dessert is originally from Italy, where it is known as crema caramella. Somalis use cardamom instead of vanilla. Before you start this recipe, make sure you have a saucepot large enough for your bundt cake pan to fit inside.*

6 heaping tablespoons sugar

4 large eggs, room temperature

1½ cups whole milk

½ teaspoon ground cardamom

⅛ teaspoon salt

Place 4 heaping tablespoons of sugar in the bottom of a bundt cake pan on a stove top on medium heat. Completely melt the sugar until it becomes honey colored. Remove from heat. Swirl sugar ⅓ up the sides of the pan. Use a spoon to coat the center of the pan with sugar.

Froth the eggs in a large mixing bowl with a hand mixer for 3 minutes. Add milk and froth another minute. Add the cardamom, salt and remaining sugar and froth a final minute.

Place 1 inch of water in the bottom of a large stockpot and bring to a rolling boil.

Pour egg mixture into the bundt cake pan. Tightly cover the pan with aluminum foil. Carefully pierce the foil in the center of the pan and wrap around the inner edge to seal. Cut 4 small, equally spaced slits in the foil.

Place the pan into the stockpot with the boiling water, cook uncovered 30 minutes or until a knife placed into the custard comes out clean.

Remove from the stockpot and uncover. Allow to cool for 5 minutes. Place a plate upside down over the top of the bundt cake pan and quickly flip to allow the cake to drop onto the plate.

Cover and chill in refrigerator for 1 hour or in a freezer for 30 minutes.

Serves 8 to 10

SUDAN

With more than 2 million dead, 4.4 million uprooted and severe food shortages, even relief agencies think twice about entering Sudan. Southern rebels and northern government forces have fought over oil and religion for more than 19 years in Africa's largest country. Both the army and the rebels abduct children to fight. Farmers and shepherds are massacred and tortured. Even relief workers are attacked. From the green Nuba mountains to the immense, dry Sahara, Sudan remains a deadly land of extremes, a nation where life is lived for the moment. And the moment is often all anyone has.

"Our wasted days are the days we never laugh."
Sudanese proverb

Sara Musa's Michigan living room is filled with boxes, emotion and irony. Her daughter Tahani has been crying. Her son Mohamed asking all morning if they really have to leave.

And Sara? After fleeing certain death in Sudan, the poverty of refugee ghettos in Cairo, and the challenge of resettlement in America, Sara simply smiles.

Sara is on the move again. And it's no surprise to her that the family is leaving for Washington, D.C.

Lansing was her place to heal. In Washington, she will again begin the fight. One day, soon, Sara will lead a women's organization in the nation's capital. Like she did in Sudan. Like she did in Egypt. *I am a woman,* she says. *I have to work among the women so we can improve ourselves and get our rights.*

It's that simple. If you are not living for your beliefs, you need to make a change.

It's important to live.

It's been a long road back to the place where Sara can say that.

In the early 1980s, Sara Musa was living a cosmopolitan Sudanese life. Her husband, Osman, was rising through the ranks of the national police with connections with Interpol and travels to Saudi Arabia, India, Iraq and Egypt.

Sara was getting connected in another way. One day she would become the head of the Khartoum branch of the National Women's Union in the capital.

The couple had seven children, four cars, three drivers, two maids and seven homes, plus an apartment in Egypt. Sara would organize protests for women's rights in secret. Osman would organize police security for the protests. After, the family would sit down for dinner together. They talked of democracy, art, culture. They talked of life.

By 1999, all that had changed. Osman was dead, assassinated by government forces. Sara's two eldest sons were missing. She had fled for her own life with internal injuries and traumatic stress from torture. More than 2 million people in her country had been killed in a civil war and 4 million had fled, including thousands to the United States. Both sides in the conflict were abducting children for battle. The life of yesterday was a memory. Sara and her family were refugees.

◆　　◆　　◆

Her path to America started years before all that. In 1983, the National Islamic Front took power and the government began sliding toward totalitarianism and genocide as it fought for control of oil in the Christian and Animist south. There seemed to be no place for the democratic ideals of the family in Khartoum. They tried to fit in. But it didn't work.

In 1989, Osman had a disagreement with a new Minister of Internal Affairs and came home sick from a trip to the Egyptian border. He died that night. Experts later said he had been poisoned.

Sara was devastated. But she didn't run. She couldn't. It wasn't time.

They were taking young boys from the streets—boys the same age as my sons ... to die in the south, she says. *It was wrong what they were doing. It was against the principles of the women's union.*

Sara organized. She led protests. She believed this: *If women ran the world, there would be no war.*

So when government agents told her to stop her work or suffer, Sara didn't stop. In 1997, the women's union in a group of 150 women marched a letter containing evidence of forced conscription of children to a United Nations official in Khartoum.

When we walked out of his office they were waiting for us.

The women were beaten by a government mob, taken to jail and tortured. Most were released, but Sara was taken to a government hospital when her brain began to swell from internal head injuries. A doctor there told her he would make sure she never got out alive. Sara refused treatment and bribed her way out of detention.

Sara's flowing traditional dress, gold rings and bracelets exemplify her strong sense of dignity.

I still never thought I would leave. I had more work to do.

Injured, Sara continued her work. She was followed. Agents maintained vigils outside her last home. One night she saw an agent making a map of the home.

They were going to come to kill me, kill my children.

Sara told the government she was going to Egypt to get treatment for her head. She took four of her children with her. Another fled to the United Arab Emirates. The government kept two sons as insurance. She has not seen them since.

In Egypt, Sara was a hero. In America, Sara is unknown. Another refugee trying to learn English. In Lansing, she has stayed home. The injuries were too much. She misses her sons.

◆   ◆   ◆

And she would do it all over again.

I was not only following my husband. I played a role. I was part of it. I was frightened. But I lived what happened in Sudan.

Her children are crying, her living room strewn with boxes.

And Sara seems happy.

She sits among the packing papers in a long, traditional gown, her jewelry glinting in the light of a single lamp, a smile on her face.

Sara has returned. Tomorrow she will go to the capital. A leader of women.

It's important to live.

Crushed red chili peppers are a staple in Sudanese cooking.

Sudanese
Culture & Cuisine

Before the battles, before the long lines of refugees trekking south to Kenya or north to Egypt, food in Sudan was as varied and rich as its cultures and climate. The nation is an extremely diverse country with no fewer than 600 distinct tribal groups speaking more than 400 languages.

In the north, where the country's majority Arab population lives, the food once reflected its Middle Eastern heritage. In the south, before it was decimated by drought and war, cattle once provided the livelihood for 40 percent of the people. Meat dishes predominated.

Yet the elders have a saying: *When two elephants fight, the grass suffers.*

And today, with the war, the food also suffers.

Ask a Sudanese youth in Grand Rapids, Michigan, or San Jose, California, what was for dinner at Kakuma, the United Nations camp established south of Sudan in Kenya, and you will get a recipe full of rice, lentils, oil and salt—the few staples passed out by the U.N. In the north, traditional meals have been equally interrupted by drought, famine and war.

In Sara's U.S. home, old northern Khartoum traditions are followed. The family sits on cushions at a low central table. Main dishes are laid out and scooped up communal style without personal plates or silverware. Instead, the Sudanese use Kisra, a pancake-like flat bread common throughout the horn of Africa. *When we sit to eat, it's a big love,* says Sara. *Food helps us to live.*

Dinner starts with soup—often Lamb and Peanut Soup, served in small cups. Main courses are laid out along with individual salads, perhaps made from cucumbers and yogurt, along with Shata, a hot sauce accompaniment on the table at every Sudanese meal.

Chai, a black tea steeped in hot milk, is served at every meal, as is an elaborate Sudanese coffee called Guhwah.

Kisra
Flat Bread

Flat breads, such as Kisra and its Ethiopian cousin injera, are used to sop up dishes served communally throughout the Horn of Africa. Sudanese make Kisra with their own yeast starter reserved from previous batters. The starter is extremely difficult to create from scratch. So, we give an easy version of Injera from the cookbook "Extending the Table." We've tasted Sara's Kisra. This is as close as one can get without the starter.

1½ **cups self-rising flour**

¼ **cup whole-wheat flour**

¼ **cup cornmeal or masa harina**

½ **tablespoon active dry yeast (½ a package)**

2¼ **cups water**

Mix the flours, cornmeal, yeast and 1¾ cups of water in a large bowl. Cover with a towel and let stand for an hour, or until the batter rises and becomes stretchy.

After the batter has risen, stir to combine any remaining water. Whip batter in a blender, adding the remaining ½ cup of water a little at a time until the batter has become quite thin—almost like pancake batter.

Pour ½ cup of the batter onto a 12-inch non-stick frying pan preheated on medium to medium-high heat. Quickly swirl the pan to spread the batter as thin as possible—no more than ⅛ of an inch. Cook until bubbles appear all over the top and the batter appears dry, or about 1 minute. Do not flip the bread.

Lay the injera on a towel for about a minute. Then place it in a covered dish to keep warm. Repeat the process until all of the batter is used.

Makes 6 12-inch breads

Salatet Zabady Bil Ajur
Cucumber Salad

*S*udanese salads are served in small personal bowls for each diner. This simple salad is Sara's favorite. It is a nice cooling balance to the heat of some Sudanese dishes.

1 **large cucumber, peeled, seeded and shredded or finely diced**

2 **cups plain yogurt**

1 **clove garlic, crushed**

salt to taste

pepper to taste

Combine all ingredients in a medium bowl. Mix thoroughly. Chill the salad at least two hours. Add salt and pepper to taste just prior to serving.

Serves 6 to 8

Maschi
Beef-Stuffed Tomatoes

The cinnamon mixed with tomatoes in this delicious main course demonstrates how Sudan blends Middle Eastern cuisine with the spices of the Orient and the vegetables of the New World. Sara says you can also stuff red, green and yellow peppers for this dish.

  1 **cup cooked rice**

  2 **pounds lean beef, chopped**

  2 **teaspoons salt, divided**

  ½ **teaspoon pepper**

  3 **cloves garlic, minced**

  4 **tablespoons fresh dill, chopped**

  4 **tablespoons olive oil**

  8 **large, firm tomatoes**

  2 **tablespoons butter**

  2 **6-ounce cans tomato paste**

1½ **cups water**

  1 **teaspoon cinnamon**

  1 **medium tomato, sliced (optional)**

  ½ **cup sliced green olives (optional)**

Saute the beef with the salt, pepper, 2 cloves of garlic, dill and 2 tablespoons of oil in a 12-inch skillet over medium/high heat until the beef has browned. Add rice. Mix thoroughly. Set aside to cool.

Cut the tops off of the tomatoes and then slit across the center with a sharp knife. Squeeze the sides of the tomatoes to open. Carefully scoop out the tomato flesh with a spoon. Be careful not to break the skin or allow the walls of the tomato to become too thin (about ¼-inch). Carefully stuff the hollowed tomatoes with the beef mixture. Set aside.

(CONTINUED ON THE NEXT PAGE)

(Maschi continued)

Warm the butter and the remaining oil in a 9-inch skillet over medium heat. Saute the tomatoes one at a time by carefully rolling them in the skillet. The tomatoes will brighten in color as they are cooked. Remove the tomatoes and arrange them, tops up, in a 6-quart saucepot. Set aside.

Combine the tomato paste, water, salt, cinnamon and remaining garlic in a bowl. Pour sauce around the tomatoes in the saucepot. Simmer on medium/low for 10 to 15 minutes until the sauce darkens.

Garnish with the tomato slices and top with the green olives.

Serves 8

Shata
Sudanese Hot Sauce

D*iners are traditionally given their own small bowls and spoons for this red-hot, lemon sauce, which intensifies the hot and sour taste of the food.*

1 **cup lemon juice
   (about 4 lemons)**

3 **cloves garlic, crushed**

3 **tablespoons red pepper
   flakes**

1 **teaspoon black pepper**

1 **teaspoon salt**

Combine ingredients in a medium bowl. Mix thoroughly. Serve chilled.

Yields about 1 cup

Shorba
Lamb and Peanut Soup

Many Sudanese meals start off with this zesty soup that features the tangy sweet and sour combinaton that is the essence of Middle Eastern and northern Sudanese cooking. Most Sudanese use lamb bones (rack of lamb or leg of lamb will do) that were previously stripped of their meat for other recipes.

3 pounds lamb bones (or lean beef ribs)

3 quarts water

2 teaspoons salt

½ pound sweet yellow onions (⅔ medium onion), chopped

½ pound carrots (about 3 large carrots), peeled and chunked

½ pound cabbage (¼ medium cabbage), cut into wedges

3 cloves garlic, minced

4 tablespoons peanut butter

3 tablespoons lemon juice

½ cup cooked rice

salt to taste

pepper to taste

Simmer the bones, water and salt in an 8-quart saucepot over medium/low heat for 1 hour or until meat has separated from the bones and has created a nice broth. Chill overnight.

The next day, use a large spoon to remove hardened fat from lamb mixture and discard. Reheat soup and add onions, carrots, cabbage and garlic. Simmer for 1 hour.

Remove the bones, let cool for 10 minutes, puree mixture and strain. You may have to do this in batches. Return soup to the saucepan, add peanut butter, lemon juice and rice. Reheat and stir until peanut butter is dissolved. Add salt and pepper to taste.

Serves 8

CUBA

People have fled Cuba ever since a former baseball player and young lawyer named Fidel Castro and his band of revolutionaries ended a dictatorial regime through three years of guerilla warfare. It was the dictator himself, Fulgencio Batista, who fled the island with $40 million in cash and a network of supporters. Then, increasingly, the people of Cuba began to flee, as Castro, now "president" for more than 44 years, clamped down on freedoms and democratic movements. Today, more than 20,000 Cubans flee for the United States each year. More than 3,000 of them are refugees escaping from political persecution. The rest are beneficiaries of "wet-foot, dry-foot," a U.S. policy that allows Cubans who make landfall across the shark-infested Florida Straits to stay. Those intercepted at sea by U.S. authorities are returned to Cuba.

> **"A revolution is a struggle to the death between the future and the past."**
>
> CUBAN DICTATOR FIDEL CASTRO

She came from the perfect Havana family and so did he. The right connections. The right ambitions. The right family values. *The family always comes first,* she says.

And they made the perfect communists. Good grades in nursing school. Members of the Union of Young Communists. Her love for the sick. His search for a cure for cancer. The perfect communist couple.

But, with time, the perfect revolution created the perfect dissident out of her: A dissident with no other choice.

But that came later. The roots, in a manner of speaking, had long been planted. *The family always comes first.* All the decisions were made. It wasn't a matter of choice.

♦　　　♦　　　♦

In the beginning, the way she tells it, it was the fog in 1984 that swept Zohiris Aguilar Calleja to Leonel Morejon Almagro. It's true, she was already in love with him. She knew it the first day he came late to class at nursing school. He was always late.

But more than that she remembers the early morning fog misting through the palms at the state work farm where they worked together. That is what swept her to Leonel Morejon Almagro. The Brazilian Roberto Carlos crooning on the radio. The secret mornings with Leonel. In 1984, the past was sweeping toward a compulsory future, the fog shrouding the mornings white during those 46 workdays. The 46 workdays on the farm made compulsory for every perfect communist by Castro. The die had been cast, so to speak. And it swept Zohiris to Leonel in a fog as compulsory as Castro could have ever made it.

And, as it was, it was all routine in the eyes of the state. The eyes that watched and reported back downtown to Havana. Back to the leaders of the revolution. Sure, Leonel ran a little organization, Naturaleza, working for a green Cuba. They planted a few trees. Ran a few campaigns. Those had certainly raised a few eyebrows. Sure he had convinced his neighbors to sign a letter he sent to Ronald Reagan criticizing "Star Wars" without approval from the party. But Leonel was young. The young get ahead of themselves.

As a couple, in the eyes of the state, they were perfect communists. By the time they were married, Leonel had dropped out of nursing school, studied law and was moving up in a well-regarded Havana firm. Zohiris had worked her way up in the health ministry and was attending conferences around the world. A beautiful little girl, Leiris Morejon Aguilar, was born. There was nothing to report. Routine stuff. Required paperwork. Little else.

Then, Leonel began to defend the wrong people—in the eyes of the state, that is. That is, Leonel and Zohiris, the perfect communists, didn't really know that defending dissidents was wrong. How could they? The Cuban Constitution, signed, sealed and delivered by the very same state under whose eyes they were so carefully watched, made it clear. Cuba is an independent and sovereign state "for the enjoyment of political freedom, social justice, individual and collective welfare, and human solidarity." That is, in the minds of Leonel and Zohiris, everyone, even dissidents, should get an adequate defense. Simple beliefs. The basis of law.

Leonel would one day be nominated for the Nobel Peace Prize, twice, on this basis. Still, Zohiris was concerned. It could attract attention. That is, attention in the eyes of the state.

I thought that maybe this is not so normal.

Then there was a knock at the door. And it was not so normal.

♦   ♦   ♦

It makes no difference who was behind the door. Or what they looked like. Or the papers they carried. Their message is always the same in times of repression. *Make a choice. Drop your husband or drop your party card.*

Zohiris dropped her card. When it comes to the state, to the party or the family, there is no choice. The decision had already been made long ago. They were the perfect couple first. The perfect Communist part was compulsory.

They made a dissident out of me. I never had said anything against the revolution.

Zohiris was fired. The trips abroad were cancelled. She was one to be watched. And, for that, Zohiris went at them.

This had become a family matter. The family always comes first.

And, as a family, Zohiris and Leonel began to dissent strongly—despite the knocks at the door. The threats of jail. In 1996, under Leonel's guidance, with Zohiris supporting, all of the opposition groups in Cuba were brought together in opposition to the state. They called it the Concilio Cubano. The Cuban Coalition. This was the first time. This was historic.

Leonel went to jail.

So, as it was, Zohiris found herself out of a job, a daughter to feed, knocks at the door and her husband in jail. She took over the organization. She kept it going. She kept strong through the last knock at the door. *You stay in Cuba, he'll get 20 years on one side of this island and you will get 20 years on the other side.*

She faced weeks in a Cuban detention center, with her chin up, despite a cell shared with a murderer. She kept strong, three weeks pregnant, through their release to U.S. authorities and the flight through Miami as refugees. She stayed strong on into her job as a seamstress. She's held it together through the birth of Leonel Morejon Aguilar, an American.

◆　　　◆　　　◆

And she's crying now as she says this in the small, sublevel apartment on a nondescript block in a middle American city. She's crying because, like all of us, she wants to go home. But she can't. And the reason is as clear as the fog sweeping through the palms in 1984. She was the perfect communist. She was the perfect dissident.

I did it for him, for my husband, my love. It's a question of love. I did it simply for love. For my family.

And my life changed completely.

My life changed completely.

Cuban
Culture & Cuisine

Cuba is world renowned for its handmade cigars.

"Love enters through the kitchen."
CUBAN SAYING

Food in Cuba, like the island nation's music and temperament, is a spicy mix of its African slave and Spanish colonial heritage. African slaves brought drums and the Santeria culture of deified saints—each worshipped with its own dish. The Spanish brought flamenco, garbanzo beans and yellow rice. Every town, as in Europe, has its own favorite plate. *The kitchen and music is who we are,* says Zohiris' husband Leonel. *It's open. It's warm. It's happy.*

And it has changed dramatically through the years. For decades, Cuban food, particularly in the capital Havana, was heavy with meat and expensive spices. Slow-cooked pork and beans, steaks and lots of oils were all part of the diet. But Castro, the revolution and the U.S. blockade-fueled economic crisis have changed all that.

Gone are the garbanzo beans, bacon and cheese of the Batista regime. Today, meals often are rice, beans and whatever cooks can find. This makes the Cuban diet incredibly varied and low on additives, since most fruits, vegetables and spices come from back yards.

Each woman had to reinvent Cuban food with what she could find, Zohiris says. Cuban women invented stuffed foods that made simple staples seem like feasts. They created new versions of fish, pork and potatoes that no longer relied on the addition of expensive spices.

During Cuba's "special period"—a time of additional belt-tightening called for by Castro in 1993, Cuban food was reinvented yet again. No meat in the market? Cuban women invented "bistec toroja," grapefruit steaks, which are exactly that.

While you likely won't find grapefruit steaks on refugee tables in the U.S., you will find flavorful food made with the freshest ingredients.

Our tradition begins in the kitchen, says Zohiris. *When we sit down at the table we are back in Cuba.*

Yucca con Mojo
Lemon & Garlic Yucca

Starchy yucca—also known as casava root or manioc—can be found grilled, boiled or fried all over Latin American. Boiled and covered with Mojo—a stock Cuban marinade of lemon, oil and garlic—yucca becomes a buttery-tasting Caribbean side dish. Yucca is becoming more widely available at large supermarkets, but you might also find it frozen at Mexican markets. Don't throw out any leftovers of this dish—if you have them. Fried Yucca con Mojo is delicious. Let it sit overnight, cut the yucca pieces in half, deep fry them in vegetable oil and serve with eggs for breakfast.

1 **2-foot yucca, peeled, halved lengthwise, cut into 3-inch lengths**

2 **teaspoons salt**

3 **cloves garlic, crushed**

1 **tablespoon extra virgin olive oil**

1 **lemon**

Boil the yucca with salt and enough water to cover it in a 6-quart saucepot for 1 hour. Drain. Remove the hard core from each piece and discard. Place on a serving platter and squeeze the juice from the lemon over the yucca.

Fry the garlic with olive oil in a small skillet until browned. Drizzle the garlic oil over the yucca.

Serves 6 to 8

Puerco Asado
Marinated Pork Roast

Throughout the Spanish-speaking Caribbean, Puerco Asado can be very elaborate. The ultimate is a marinated pig slow-roasted over an open fire for 12 hours. This is Zohiris' time-saving version and the family's favorite. Cubans use the marinade on just about any meat, though Zohiris prefers pork shoulder. The key ingredient, orange marinating sauce, comes from the juice of the bitter orange and is sold by Mi Costenita or Goya at Mexican food markets.

2 **pounds pork, cut into 4-inch pieces**

1 **cup orange marinating sauce**

4 **cloves of garlic, crushed**

⅓ **pound sweet yellow onions (½ cup), finely chopped**

1 **teaspoon dried oregano**

⅓ **tablespoon extra virgin olive oil**

salt to taste

Mix pork, orange marinating sauce, garlic, onion and oregano in a non-metal bowl, cover and marinate at room temperature for ½ hour.

Cover the bottom of a 6-quart saucepot with olive oil on medium heat. Add the pork and fry slowly until it is golden brown.

Add the marinade and enough water to the pot to just cover the pork. Bring to a rolling boil. Reduce heat and simmer on low for about 15 minutes or until the water and marinade have cooked into a thick sauce. Add salt to taste.

Serve with Black Beans and Rice.

Serves 4

Frijol Negro con Arroz
Black Beans and Rice   (*SEE PHOTOGRAPH ON NEXT PAGE*)

Some Cubans add chicken or pork fat to their black beans. But this vegetarian version of Zohiris' is the essence of tasty but basic, post-Castro, Cuban cooking. It works great as a side dish or even a main course.

9 cups cooked rice

4 cups dry black beans

1 tablespoon olive oil

⅓ pound green pepper (1 cup), chopped

½ head of garlic, minced

1 teaspoon oregano

1 teaspoon cumin

1 bay leaf

salt to taste

Rinse the beans and place in a medium bowl with enough water to cover the beans. Soak overnight, adding water if necessary.

Stirring frequently, fry the pepper, garlic, oregano, cumin and bay leaf in the olive oil in a 6-quart saucepot on medium-low heat. The peppers should become soft and the garlic browned.

Add the soaked beans and their water. Bring to a boil. Reduce heat and simmer for about 45 minutes or until the beans are medium soft and the water has turned into a thick sauce. Add more water as necessary to keep the beans from burning on the bottom.

Add salt to taste. Serve over rice.

Serves 6 to 8

Frijol Negro con Arroz
See recipe previous page

Boniatillo
Sweet Potato Pudding

Every Cuban cook has his or her own version of this popular, creamy dessert. Some versions are extremely elaborate and call for sherry and eggs. Boniatillo is traditionally made at Christmas time. In Cuba, white sweet potatoes, common to the island, are used. They say you can find them occasionally at Mexican markets, but we couldn't. Still, Zohiris' version, made with domestic yellow sweet potatoes, is one of the most delicious, easy-to-make desserts we've tasted.

1 **pound sweet potatoes (2½ cups), peeled and cut into 1-inch cubes**

4 **cups whole milk**

1 **cup sugar**

½ **teaspoon cinnamon**

¼ **teaspoon salt**

Boil the sweet potatoes in a 2-quart saucepot until soft. Drain, return to the saucepot and mash.

Add milk, sugar, cinnamon and salt.

Stirring constantly, cook on medium to medium-low heat for 45 minutes or until it thickens into a bright orange, creamy pudding.

Chill covered for 2 hours.

Serves 6 to 8

AFGHANISTAN

Located at the crossroads of Central Asia, Afghanistan has seen war among its people and invasions by outsiders for much of its history. In 1979, the Soviet Union invaded Afghanistan, sending millions fleeing to Pakistan and Iran. The Soviets withdrew in 1988 after nearly a decade of U.S.-supported, mujahedeen resistance. The U.S. quickly dropped their support, and the nation lapsed into an eight-year civil war. The Taliban, created in Pakistan refugee camp religious schools, took power in 1996. With its extreme interpretation of Islamic law, the Taliban ruled Afghanistan and Afghan refugee camps harshly. And today, after the invasion of the country by a United States searching for Osama bin Laden, many refugee women remain in danger of Taliban persecution in Afghanistan and refugee camps in Pakistan.

She says it as a matter of fact.
I can't find my sister.
A fact. A statement. As if Wasima is telling time.
It's 9:42 a.m. Today is Friday.
I can't find my sister. She was my best friend.
In America, we try to ignore these statements. We want to hear about freedom and rescues and happy endings. But it's the facts that matter to Wasima.
The deaths. The escapes. The near misses. These are the creaks and groans that fill the homes we try to build. The dust in rooms none of us should see.
These are facts.
I can't find my sister. She was my best friend.
These facts can't be ignored. They surround us.

♦   ♦   ♦

Wasima's brother Tooryalai clicks on a keyboard at a refugee development center. This is what he says:
Where can you get cheap computer? But good like this one? How do you

chat? What about internet hook up? How much I pay?

We shrug.

You know, I saw my brother killed one day. We had escaped from the Taliban. They shot him in the back. I went back to save him. I couldn't carry him. I was captured. He is dead.

◆   ◆   ◆

These details leave no room for escape. What is freedom? What is a rescue? What is a happy ending?

We are all crying at Wasima's house.

All the stories are sad.

The first time we all meet, we have cameras at the ready, batteries charged, pencils sharpened. And they? They have their memories: escape from the Taliban, threats in Pakistan, resettlement in Michigan.

The house is immaculate. Almonds are on the table. Tea is in our hands. Everyone gathers on the couches.

Zuleikha, 14. Storay, 17. Wasima, 19. Tooryalai, 29.

Nafisa, the mom. Hajishahagha, the dad.

No last names, please. It is too dangerous.

I don't ask much more after that.

Because not everyone is on the couch.

Zohal, 18, Wasima's best friend and sister: missing in Pakistan or Europe.

Spogmay, 22, sister: lost in a bomb blast in Kabul.

Wahzma, 25, sister: lost in a bomb blast in Kabul.

Baryalai, 26, brother: killed while fleeing the Taliban.

Ngyalai, 27, brother: fled to Iran, missing.

But all of them are there. In the room. In the air. Mom is crying.

And we learn this that night: Wasima holds the family together.

Wasima takes care of her father, who is sick. High blood pressure, diabetes. A bullet wound in his foot. Wasima gives him medicine. They go for morning walks.

Wasima's mother is depressed and works long hours. She misses her children. Tooryalai was beaten for months. He forgets. He has headaches. Wasima cleans. She shops. Zuleikha and Storay are too young to remember what happened. They study constantly.

Sometimes Wasima downloads pictures of Indian movie stars on the Internet. She longs to be an interior decorator.

Most of the time Wasima cooks. *It's for me. I want them to say "It's so delicious that I want to eat my five fingers."*

Wasima's favorite dish is Chicken Chow Mein.

◆   ◆   ◆

The next time we visit, Wasima's hands are full of flour. She is flinging it at Storay. They are laughing. Out of fear or fun, Wasima won't tell us when we can next meet to talk about the facts. The details. And she won't let us leave without food.

But one day we call her. She says come over.

The house is dark. It is just Storay to translate the facts.

These are facts:

There was always bombing in Kabul. As long as I can remember. Some bombs, you could stay at home and hide. Other bombs, you must run. Mom screamed: "Get out of here." It was the other bombs. I ran and ran. Spogmay and Wahzma never came back. They were 13 and 14.

My Daddy gave Ngyalai money to flee to Iran. He said he couldn't take it anymore. We never saw Ngyalai again.

The Taliban wanted my daddy to put up a white flag on our house. That meant he had girls marrying age. They said marrying age was 10 years old. My daddy refused to put up the flag. Zuleikha never left our house until we left for Pakistan in 1999. I went out twice. I put my Burka on backwards both times. I could only stare at the ground.

The Taliban wanted money from my daddy. He refused. They said to my daddy, "You will come with us." My brothers fought with the Taliban. They took all three away. My daddy, Tooryalai and Baryalai. They decided to teach my daddy a lesson. They shot him in his toes and sent my daddy back home. That was in 1999. We fled for Pakistan. Zohal's husband wouldn't let her come with us to America. She may be in Europe. No one knows what happened. No one knew then what happened to my brothers.

It was the end of December 2000. Baryalai and Tooryalai tried to escape. They were being held in the basement of a house. It was like a basement. They got to the street. They shot Baryalai five times in the back. Tooryalai tried to carry him. They caught him. He was beaten. Put in jail. He was beaten more and was put in a hospital. He escaped after September 11th.

What happened that night—the night Tooryalai found Wasima and the family in Pakistan?

I remember it very well. It was 11:30 at night. He knocked on the door. He said, "Mommy it's me." We were so happy. We hugged him. He was crying. We were crying. Then he said, "Mommy, I'm sorry. Baryalai didn't make it."

We were so sad.

♦　　♦　　♦

We were all crying at Wasima's house.

These are the facts.

And all the stories are sad.

Afghan women take great pride in their handmade clothes and jewelry, such as these silver earrings.

Afghan
Culture & Cuisine

Afghanistan's food demonstrates the nation's status as a crossroads between Asia and the Middle East. The staples—tandori oven-baked flatbread and black, cardamom-laced tea, called nan and chai respectively—are also found in India. Many festival foods—the meatball-based Kofta and charbroiled lamb Kabobs—are straight from the Middle East.

Yet some foods, such as the potato and onion-filled Bolawnee are inherently Afghan. Many meals in Afghanistan are eaten with Pilau, a white rice that has been flavored with vegetables and spices.

Breakfast is usually dried cheese and chai. There is no sit down meal for lunch. Instead, nuts and fruits are eaten throughout the day.

In most Afghan homes, including Wasima's, families sit down together for dinner, with the women serving the men. No utensils are used. Diners scoop food with their right hands (left hands are reserved for sanitary functions), sometimes using a piece of nan to grab the food. They then push the bites into their mouths using their thumbs.

Desserts are usually of the perfumed variety, such as firni, a custard flavored with rose water and cardamom.

It's important to note that the very ingredients many native-born Americans see as representative of a poor diet—sugar, grease and oil—are signs of affluence in impoverished, war-torn Afghanistan. While daily foods—nan, chai, fruits and vegetables—are very low in fat and sugars, festival foods come in copious quantities and often with a thick sheen of grease and oil.

For the Qabuli Pilau recipe, we have added an additional step to remove much of the fat. To truly experience this traditional festival food of Afghanistan, leave it in and enjoy.

Bolawnee
Fried Potato and Onion Pastries

Similar to the irresistible fried pastries of southern India, this appetizer made with wheat flour and stuffed with potatoes and onions is a favorite of Wasima and her family. Many Afghans use fried leeks in place of the potatoes and onions and spice up the filling with crushed red peppers.

4 cups flour

2 tablespoons salt

1 tablespoon active dry yeast

1¾ cups warm water

2 pounds potatoes (4½ cups), chopped

2 pounds sweet yellow onions (4½ cups), peeled and diced

¼ cup vegetable oil

vegetable oil for frying

Sift the flour into a very large mixing bowl. Mix 1 tablespoon salt, yeast and water thoroughly in a small bowl and add to the flour, while mixing with a fork. Knead into a smooth dough that does not stick to your hands. Add more flour or water as necessary. Set aside for 10 minutes.

Boil the potatoes until soft. Drain and mash them with the remaining salt in a large bowl.

Fry the onions in ¼-cup of oil until they begin to turn brown. Mix the onions with the mashed potatoes.

Cut the dough into eight equal-sized balls. Take a ball, stretch and roll it into a thin circle, about 8 to 12 inches in diameter. Spread ⅛ of the filling across the circle of dough, leaving 2 inches of it uncovered along the edges. Fold the circle in half and press the pastry closed with your thumb.

Warm about an inch of oil in a 12-inch skillet over medium to medium/high heat. Carefully place the pastry into the oil and fry until golden brown. Alternatively, fry in a lightly oiled, non-stick skillet. Turn the pastry occasionally to ensure it is evenly fried. Drain and cool on a paper towel. Repeat with the rest of dough and filling.

Serve with Cilantro & Chile Chutney. (See recipe on the next page.)

Yields 8 pastries

Chatni
Cilantro & Chile Chutney

Reflecting their ties to the sub-continent, Afghans serve chutney—a chunky relish that may be sweet or hot—as a condiment at every meal. This zesty garlic, chile and cilantro version is Wasima's favorite. It goes great on Bolawnee. In fact, it goes great on just about everything. Afghans serve it with plain yogurt to cut the heat for those that need it.

1 large bunch cilantro
4 cloves garlic
1-2 Thai green chiles
1 cup white vinegar
3 walnut halves
salt to taste

Chop all of ingredients in a blender or food processor until they make a chunky sauce.

Yields 2 cups

KOFTA WA CHALOW

Kofta wa Chalow
Meat Patties in Sauce

Almost every culture and country from Morocco to India has a version of Kofta. These Middle Eastern meat patties have many different spellings and are prepared in many different ways. Some Koftas are grilled. Others are broiled or baked. In this recipe, the meat is boiled along with blended tomatoes and coriander—a staple spice in Afghanistan—to make a rich sauce. Wasima suggests serving it with Qabuli Pilau (page 58).

1½ **pounds sweet yellow onions (3¾ cups), chopped**

1 **head garlic, minced**

3 **tablespoons vegetable oil**

3 **pounds ground chuck (or other lean ground beef)**

1 **tablespoon coriander**

1 **teaspoon black pepper**

1 **tablespoon salt**

1 **egg**

water

4 **very ripe tomatoes, blended**

salt to taste

Fry 2½ cups of onion and the garlic in 2 tablespoons vegetable oil in a 12-inch skillet until onions turn translucent. Mince the onion and garlic mixture in a food processor or blender. Mix the onion and garlic thoroughly with ground chuck, coriander, black pepper, salt and egg. Form the mixture into compact balls about the size of golf balls. Flatten them into fat patties. Set aside.

Fry the remaining onions in 1 tablespoon of vegetable oil in a 12-inch skillet until the onions become translucent. Mince the onions in a food processor and pour into a 6-quart saucepot. Stack the meat patties in the saucepot with the onions, ensuring that both are evenly mixed. Add water until it just barely covers the top patties. Boil uncovered for 30 minutes or until the water is nearly gone, skimming the fat from the surface. Add the tomatoes and boil until the sauce has deepened to a dark brownish-red. Add salt to taste during this process. Do not stir with a utensil, it will break the patties apart. Instead, shake the pot horizontally across the burner to mix.

Serves 6 to 8

Qabuli Pilau
Flavored Rice with Lamb

*K*abuli is a term urban Afghans use if they want to refer to people from the capital without bringing up the ethnic divisions that have kept the country in a state of war, some say, for centuries. But Qabuli is Afghanistan's signature dish, loosely translated as "Food of the Kings." Afghans love to eat mountainous amounts during festivals and celebrations. Traditionally they will heap it on a platter and keep it coming until no one can move.

1½ **pounds sweet yellow onions (3¾ cups), diced**

1 **cup vegetable oil**

4 **pounds leg of lamb, cut into 2-inch cubes**

1 **heaping tablespoon tomato paste**

3 **Thai green chiles or jalapeños, cut in half lengthwise**

3 **teaspoons salt**

3 **quarts plus ¾ cup water**

4 **cups uncooked, aromatic long-grain basmati rice**

2 **tablespoons cumin**

6 **ounces almond spears (1½ cups)**

12 **ounces carrots (2 cups), julienned**

6 **ounces raisins, (1 cup)**

Fry 2½ cups of onions in ⅓-cup oil in an 8-quart pressure cooker (no rack) on high heat until the onions begin to brown. Add the lamb and fry with the onions on medium/high heat for about 10 minutes. While the lamb and onions are frying, mix the tomato paste with enough water to make a thick sauce. Reduce heat to low and add the tomato sauce, green chiles and 2 teaspoons salt. Add 4¼ cups of water and mix. Cook in a pressure cooker for 20 minutes according to the manufacturer's instructions. Cool pressure cooker under cold water to reduce pressure, remove and discard the chiles and refrigerate overnight.

The next day, skim and discard the hardened layer of fat from the top of the lamb.

Bring 8½ cups of water to a boil in an 8-quart saucepot on high heat. Add the rice and stir occasionally for about 10 minutes or until the rice is medium soft. Drain the water, reserving 2 cups for later. Return the rice to the non-stick pot and set aside.

Fry the remaining onions in ⅓-cup of oil in a large, 2-quart saucepot on medium/high heat until the onions begin to brown. Remove from heat and cool. Puree the onions in a blender. Return to the pot along with the 2 cups of water that were reserved after draining the rice. Bring this to a boil and add the cumin and remaining salt. Boil until it has reduced to 1½ cups.

Add this sauce to the rice. Cook covered on high heat for 1 minute. Reduce heat and simmer for 15 minutes or until the rice is cooked.

While the rice is cooking, warm the lamb over medium-low heat.

Fry the almonds in 1 tablespoon vegetable oil in a 12-inch skillet on medium heat, stirring constantly, until they turn a light, golden brown. Transfer into a medium bowl.

Add a tablespoon of vegetable oil to the skillet and fry the raisins on medium heat until plump. Watch carefully. The raisins plump very quickly and can burn easily. Add to the bowl with the almonds.

Pour the remaining vegetable oil into the skillet and fry half the carrots on high heat until they pale in color. Add the fried carrots to the bowl with the almonds and raisins. Repeat with the rest of the fresh carrots.

Dish ⅔ of the rice onto a large platter and heap the lamb on top. Sprinkle the remaining rice around and on top of the lamb. Sprinkle the carrot, raisin and almond mixture on top. Serve immediately.

Serves 8 to 10.

COLOMBIA

Nicknamed "Locombia," Colombia—with its ongoing conflict between the government, drug traffickers, rebels and paramilitaries—is one of the most dangerous places in the Western Hemisphere. More than 2 million people, caught in the crossfire, have fled their homes. Tens of thousands have died in the chaos. While the U.S. does not regularly resettle refugees from Colombia, our nation's attitude toward persecution in Colombia may be changing. In 1999, less than 2 percent of all Colombian asylum applicants were actually granted this life-saving international designation by U.S. immigration officials. By 2001, that number had changed dramatically, with immigration officials granting asylum to 60 percent of all Colombian applicants.

To hear Maria Clara Jaramillo Velazquez tell it, it's as if it all were happenstance. A twist of fate, one might say.

Rebels may or may not have told her secrets she never should have heard.

The phone may or may not have rung off the hook with death threats thereafter.

She may or may not have always wanted to come to America.

She may or may not see her family again.

She may or may not have found a new friend in the most improbable place.

But it so happens that they did and it did and she has and she won't and she did.

And her life, like all lives in war, has forever changed.

◆   ◆   ◆

In 2001, the "little war" around Cali, her home city, continued to rage. The war, fought between paramilitaries, rebels and the drug cartels, burst out daily in machine gun fire and mortar rounds in the mountains.

The city had its own violence. No one was safe. Anyone could disappear. Anyone could be killed—whether or not they were involved. Even for Clara, a newly graduated resident working in a mental health ward at the central hospital, the war in 2001 was a dull, pit-of-the-stomach threat. But still a threat. Taken at face value, each death seemed a fluke, a long shot. It was that kind of war. A war of circumstance.

In September 2001, the professor she worked with as a teaching assistant was killed. It's possible he was killed by the war. The evidence, like all evidence in this war, appeared circumstantial. And it so happened that Clara's assistant disappeared a month later. Correlation to the war? Maybe. Circumstantial, definitely. It so happened, that Clara should have been next.

As luck would have it, a mental health ward at a central hospital in Colombia is a battleground. The law in Colombia says that everyone must receive treatment regardless of their activities with the war. The law in Colombia says that everyone treated must see a psychologist. The law in Colombia brought every wounded paramilitary, rebel and narco-terrorist down from the mountains to Clara.

They told me things about the war, Clara says.

Things no one should have known. Where a car bomb would occur. Where an attack would come.

Each time before they would say, "Doctora, usted sabe que se puede decir nada." Doctor, you understand that you can say nothing.

She understood. Medical ethics are like that. But more than that, a war of circumstance is like that. Head down, mouth shut. That's the rule.

Everyone knew the rule. Everyone followed the rule. It just so happened following the rules wasn't enough. Even so, Clara's explanation is clinical.

As a psychologist, I would say that they have anti-social problems. They want to control something. And I turned out to be the one they wanted to control.

Letters came to her office. Then to her home. Then came phone calls.

Now, at this point, I was scared. It's sad. Colombia is a scary, violent place. Se acostumbra. You get used to it. But now I was scared.

Clara went to the police for protection. But what could the police do? In a war of circumstance there is no protection from chance.

The police told me to write a letter for their files. They said, that way, when I was killed, they would know which group did it.

Clara fled for the United States.

She arrived on a tourist visa on Dec. 2, 2001. She spent everything she had to come. She pawned her late mother's jewelry to come. Return was no option. She would likely never see her family again. She misses them terribly.

Clara e-mails her brother Gustavo every day. *He's my life. He's in Colombia. But he's the most important person in my life.* She misses her mother, Merceditas, who died when she was 16. She misses her mourning father, Hernan, who she had just begun to get to know as an adult when she had to flee.

Missing her family, Clara spoke no English when she arrived. She had no money. She would soon have no papers. As a rule, tourist visas run out.

Clara was 23.

This was not the U.S., the Disney World, she had dreamed of as a child. There was no help. No welcome. The newspapers spoke of round-ups of illegal immigrants and their treatment as terrorists. When Clara went for English classes at a local adult education program, they asked for her social security number. She didn't know it was illegal for her to be asked. She never went back. She taught herself English instead.

The biggest problem was the lack of papers. She never considered asking for asylum.

I thought that was for presidents.

Then, by chance, she heard about a local refugee service agency that could help. The agency helped her apply for asylum and get a legal job while they waited for an answer.

That's when, by chance, Clara met one of her best new friends. Folks in the Alzheimer's Unit call her Mimi. She is 96 years old.

I am a lucky woman. My old people are the angels in my life. It's so great because they are so crazy. Most days Mimi doesn't know me when she sees me. She knows me by my voice. When I say "Hello, Mimi." She says, "Oh, you're the one who takes care of me." I just love her. One day I saw her. I said, "How are you Mimi?" She said, "I don't know. I'm confused." I said "Why Mimi?" She said, "I think I'm pregnant but I'm not sure." It's like that every day. They say something new. Something wonderful. I love her.

Meanwhile, Clara was still in danger. The government had not yet decided her case.

The attorneys at the refugee agency explained to her the subjectivity of the process, how it relied on the whims of the immigration office.

How it relied, as much as anything else really, on chance.

I was scared to death the day we went to Chicago for the decision.

The receptionist was Guatemalan. She spoke to me in Spanish. She said "Are you the Colombian?" I said, "Yes." She went for the envelope. She didn't smile.

I was so afraid.

She gave it to me. She smiled.

"Maria Clara," she said. "Felicidades. Consigo asylo."

Congratulations. You have been granted asylum.

A 60-40 chance. The whims of the immigration office. Clara's life was changed for good.

I couldn't believe it. I was just crying and crying.

Having fled without anything of value, Clara treasures this Colombian flag as a reminder of the home to which she cannot return.

Colombian
Culture & Cuisine

A mixture of indigenous groups, conquistadors, oceans and mountains have made Colombian food as varied and distinct as any in the world.

Beans and rice, Fresh Corn Cakes and yucca have been eaten for millennia by the indigenous peoples of Colombia, where 75 distinct indigenous languages are still spoken today. Clara says these foods are the basis of Colombian cuisine, itself.

In contrast, foods like Natilla, a Christmas pudding, reflect the tastes of the Europeans—part of the region's culture since the Spanish established a first permanent settlement on the South American mainland at Santa Maria la Antigua del Darien in 1510. Their ancestors are now known as "Los Paisas," a culture of old, colonial values, centered in the country's northwest. And yet, even Natilla, with its fresh coconut flavoring, reflects the variety of fruits and vegetables found throughout the country.

At the same time, Colombian food is incredibly regional. Everyone knows that Antioquian Beans come from "Los Paisas" of Medillin and Sancocho de Gallina is a chicken soup from Cali. Bogota has their own chicken and potato soup that its inhabitants call Ajiaco.

Yet, no matter how varied and regional Colombian food is, everyone eats the same way in Colombia. Clara descibes it with one word: *Sundays.*

Sundays bring together generations of families throughout Colombia to feast. More than enough food is made so that members can head home with leftovers for the week.

We are a family people. Every Sunday is very important in Colombia, she says.

Arepas de Choclo
Fresh Corn Cakes

The indigenous peoples of Colombia have been making variations of these thick, soft corn cakes for hundreds of years, particularly on the nation's Pacific coast. Today, Arepas are served with just about every Colombian dish and continue to be the central source of sustenance for the poor of Colombia. "They are sweet and delicious," says Clara. "We call them Masitas when they are made small."

4 **cobs corn**
1 **teaspoon salt**
4 **tablespoons cornstarch**
   butter to taste

Cut the corn from the cob and grind with the salt in a blender or food processor. Add cornstarch and blend. More cornstarch will result in denser cakes.

Pour the batter ¼-cup at a time onto a non-stick skillet over medium to medium-high heat. Brown on both sides.

Serve hot with butter and salt.

Serves 4 to 6

Frijoles de Antioquia
Antioquian Beans

These beans are a dish of "Los Paisas"—the rugged traditionalists of Medellin. This dynamic, industrial city, located in the state of Antioquia, northwest of Colombia's capital Bogota, is one of the largest in the country. And they do things a little different there, says Clara. Take the beans, for instance. "In my country, most of us eat everything with white rice," Clara says. "In Antioquia, they eat everything with these beans." Clara says people sometimes substitute salt pork and beef for the bacon to give the beans a different flavor. Either way, she says everyone throughout Colombia makes large pots of this dish to have leftovers for breakfast and the rest of the week. And with good reason: "I can eat Antioquian Beans all the days of my life," Clara says.

1 **pound dry kidney beans, soaked at least 4 hours**

2 **slices bacon, chopped**

1 **green plantain, finely chopped**

½ **tablespoon salt**

½ **tablespoon cooking oil**

½ **pound tomatoes (¾ cups), chopped**

½ **pound sweet yellow onions (1½ cups), chopped**

1 **clove garlic, minced**

Drain and rinse the beans.

Combine with the bacon and enough water to cover them in a pressure cooker. Cook according to the manufacturer's instructions on medium-high heat for 1 hour or until tender. Cool pressure cooker under cold water to reduce pressure.

Add the plantain and simmer uncovered on medium heat until soft. Add the salt and mix well.

Saute the tomatoes, onions and garlic in oil in a 12-inch skillet on medium heat until soft. Add to the beans and mix well.

Simmer the beans for ½ hour until all the flavors are absorbed.

Serves 8

Sancocho de Gallina
Cali Chicken Soup

(*See photograph on the next page*)

Walk through the streets of Clara's hometown, Cali, and this soup—brightened with fresh cilantro and yellow plantains—is advertised outside every restaurant. Then take a Sunday walk through the surrounding countryside, the Farallones de Cali Mountains looming nearby, and Sancocho is bubbling in pots in nearly every home. "All the farmers kill one chicken on Sunday and make this soup," Clara says. "Then everyone gathers to eat it together."

1 **bunch scallions (1 cup), coarsely chopped**

1 **bunch cilantro (1 cup), coarsely chopped**

1 **teaspoon cumin**

2 **quarts chicken broth**

2 **tablespoons flour**

2 **tablespoons butter**

3 **chicken breasts, skinned and quartered**

1 **1-foot yucca, skinned and cut into 1-inch cubes**

2 **medium red potatoes, cut into 1-inch cubes**

2 **ripe plantains, halved and sliced into thirds lengthwise**

6 **tablespoons lemon juice (about 2 lemons)**

salt to taste

pepper to taste

Simmer the scallions, cilantro and cumin in 1 cup of broth in a 1-quart saucepan for 5 minutes. Allow to cool and process in a blender until it is smooth and green. Set aside.

Simmer the flour and butter in a 1-quart saucepan over medium-high heat stirring constantly until it forms a slightly brown roux. Add one cup of broth, mix thoroughly and set aside.

Simmer the chicken, yucca and potatoes in the remaining broth in an 8-quart saucepot, ladling the fat off the top, for 30 minutes. Add the plantains and simmer for 20 minutes. Add the scallions, cilantro and cumin mixture, roux and lemon juice, mix thoroughly and simmer for an additional 10 minutes. Add water to thin if necessary.

Soup is ready when chicken is cooked all the way through and plantains are soft but not disintegrating. Add salt and pepper to taste.

Serves 6 to 8

SANCOCHO DE GALLINA
SEE RECIPE PREVIOUS PAGE

Natilla
Cinnamon and Coconut Pudding

This creamy dessert can be found in bakeries throughout Colombia anytime of the year. But on Christmas, the dessert moves up the Colombian culinary ranks to star status. "When the baby Jesus is born and put in the manger for Christmas, Natilla is everywhere," says Clara. "It's in the bakeries. People make it in their homes. They even sell it at traffic lights."

½ **quart whole milk**

¾ **cup cornstarch**

¾ **cup brown sugar**

3 **cinnamon sticks**

⅓ **pound fresh coconut (1 cup), shredded**

Dissolve the cornstarch and brown sugar in the milk in a 3-quart saucepot. Add the cinnamon and coconut and cook over low heat, stirring constantly until the pudding has thickened.

Pour into a serving dish and chill.

Serves 6 to 8

KURDISTAN

No one from Kurdistan says they are from Iraq — or any other country. Their culture reaches as far back as written records have been kept in the Middle East. But Kurdistan basically doesn't exist. Found at the intersection of Turkey, Iraq, Iran, Syria and Armenia, the history of Kurdistan is a litany of government crackdowns on its attempts to gain independence. From 1975 on, no less than 1 million Kurds have fled attempts to wipe them out. More than 200,000 have been killed. In 1996, Saddam Hussein issued a decree sentencing to death any Kurd with U.S. ties. Fearing more repression, thousands fled for Turkey and Iran for the second time in a decade and were turned back. The U.S. eventually resettled thousands of these Kurds in the United States. Today, more than 600,000 Kurds are displaced and thousands more live as refugees. Suad Finde is one of them.

She was born an American.

Not in the literal, God Bless Bruce Springsteen, Born in the USA sense of the word. No. Suad Finde took her first breath in Kurdistan, a part of Iraq few in the U.S. had heard of until the 1990s.

She was born an American in her heart. And, today, it's in her CD player with Whitney Houston, the Backstreet Boys, Britney Spears, `N Sync and Jennifer Lopez. And on her television with The Powerpuff Girls.

I don't know what it was back then, she says now. *Maybe it was the movies. Maybe it was the music. Maybe it was just me. I saw America as this open place. This free country. When I would sit with my friends or my cousins I always felt strange. Different. I was alone.*

Kurdistan, a rugged, impenetrable area of northern Iraq, is a tough place to be born an American.

First there was the threat of Saddam Hussein, the iron-fisted dictator of Iraq, to contend with. He had been trying to wrest autonomy from the Kurds for years. In 1988, when Suad was 12, nearly 200,000 Kurds were killed or disappeared by the government of Saddam Hussein.

Then there was Kurdish tradition itself.

You hear it since the day you open your eyes, explains Suad's husband, Hassan. *You have to live this particular way. You must act that particular way. For a woman like Suad in a society like that, she couldn't do anything. She couldn't say what she wanted, do what she wanted. She couldn't do anything. For a man, he can be hated for living the way he wants. But at least he won't be killed.*

The couple married after mutual family members noticed they had similar beliefs about freedom, independence, women's rights. Like most refugees, Hassan never particularly wanted, nor believed, he would one day flee for America.

But Suad had dreamed of a life in America for as long as she could remember. It took an American war against an Iraqi dictator for it to happen.

In 1991, thousands of Kurds—inspired by the success of the Americans in the first Gulf War—rose up against the government. They believed the U.S. would join in the battle and their march for independence straight to Baghdad.

The Americans didn't show up. Thousands of Kurds were killed when the Iraqi government crushed the rebellion. More than 1 million Kurds fled for the mountainous Turkish border and were turned back. Several thousand died of exposure.

We were waiting for George Bush, Suad says, recalling those two months in the mountains. *We were waiting, waiting, waiting. From that day, the Americans have always lived with us.*

The U.S., along with the United Nations, created so-called safe havens in northern Iraq and closed down the sky to Iraqi planes. Suad's husband was hired by the Kurdistan Reconstruction Organization, funded by the international community, to rebuild Kurdish cities and villages destroyed during the clashes. Then, in 1996, Saddam reacted.

Saddam announced that he would kill every single person and their families who worked with the Americans, Suad recalls. *It was on the news. It was like that for three or four months. Every day, we heard that Saddam would strike. We didn't know what would happen.*

The Americans pulled Hassan and Suad out. And once again the family was stuck on the Turkish border. Suad was pregnant. The Turks didn't want them and pushed them toward America, fueling their interest with rumors that when families such as Hassan's reached the U.S. they would get new houses, cars and $3,000.

The U.S. flew them to Guam.

We were scared to death, Suad says. *People said there were sharks. They eat*

The Koran, the central text of Islam, is kept in most Kurdish households.

people. They said you don't know what's going to happen to you. We said "Oh well, it's better than living with Saddam."

It was beautiful in Guam. It was warm. There were beaches. I was pregnant with Zana there. That's why he's so beautiful.

After four months they were relocated to the mainland U.S., where reality hit. Not all of America is Beverly Hills, new cars and `N Sync videos. Most Kurds were resettled, like the majority of refugees, with very little government assistance in small apartments in American inner cities.

We went to the refugee agency, says Suad. *We asked "Where is our $3,000, where are our cars, where are our new houses?" They said "Where did you get that idea?"*

Even harder was the isolation. After a war, a price on her head and a trip halfway around the world, Suad realized America had come with a significant cost.

I miss my family, she says. *Over there I had no freedom, but I had my family. Over here I have freedom, but no family.*

Would she go back? She has. Once. But just to visit. Her life is in America. The family is stable. Zana, now 6, is growing.

Still, while she was in Iraq, Suad had heard that a mall called Supermarket had opened in the Kurdish city of Duhok.

I had to see this.

Because, after all, she was born an American.

And do I like the mall! Oh my God, I wish I could just live in them. I wish I had $2,000 to buy it all. I see all that stuff. I like the smell of all that American food.

I missed America so much in Duhok. I had to go to that mall.

It felt like home.

Kurdish
Culture & Cuisine

"I don't love angel eyes,
Flesh white like marble.
I love rocks, mountain tops
Lost among the clouds."

FROM "I AM A KURD"
BY HEMIN, A KURDISH POET

At home in the steep, forbidding mountainous areas of Iraq, Turkey and Iran, Kurds have developed an extremely private society that relies heavily on families living tribally in deep mountain valleys.

It's a private life granted by sheer Kurdish will-power against invaders' attempts to crush their existence for millennia and against the wild extremes of the mountains—a landscape where temperatures go from -20°F in the winter to more than 100°F in the summer.

Put Kurds on flat land, say military experts, and they will certainly be defeated. Put them in the mountains and they are unbeatable.

Families are ruled by strict cultural and religious codes that govern almost every aspect of a very formal life. Though Kurdish weddings are elaborate affairs, adorned with beautiful garments and mounds of stuffed vegetables, meats and spiced rice, it's considered impolite for Kurdish men to speak of their families outside the home. The husband's mother wields inordinate power. Marriages are arranged and women are considered property of the household.

Scholars link Kurdish culture to Tajiks and Pashtuns in Afghanistan and Baluchis in Northern Pakistan, all very mountainous areas. And their food is very similar (see Afghan Culture and Cuisine on page 54).

Historically, few outsiders were allowed access to the Kurds by Iran, Iraq and Turkey, their culture has seen very little outside influence until recently.

Zlata
Kurdish Salad

This easy, fresh-tasting salad goes well with Iprach (page 78) and Bryani (page 76). It is very similar to Lebanese Fattoush salad.

- **2 pounds tomatoes (2 cups), chopped**
- **½ pound cucumber (1½ cups), chopped**
- **⅛ pound green pepper (½ cup), chopped**
- **⅛ pound sweet yellow onions (¼ cup), chopped**
- **½ pound iceberg lettuce (2 cups), shredded**
- **½ teaspoon salt**
- **4 tablespoons lemon juice**
- **2 tablespoons extra virgin olive oil**
- **½ teaspoon black pepper**

Mix ingredients in a large bowl. Serve immediately.

Serves 4 to 6

Kabobs
Skewered Beef

These easy Kabobs can be fried or grilled and served as an appetizer or a main course. Seven Spices can be found at Middle Eastern markets.

- **1½ pounds ground beef**
- **⅔ pound sweet yellow onions (1 cup), minced**
- **2 celery stalks (1 cup), minced**
- **1 tablespoon salt**
- **½ teaspoon black pepper**
- **1 teaspoon Seven Spices**
- **2 cloves garlic, minced**
- **½ cup flour**

Mix ingredients in a large bowl. Form into tightly-packed, 2-by-1-inch patties. Skewer and grill. Or fry in 2 inches of oil over medium heat until cooked through. Drain.

Serves 4 to 6.

Bryani
Spiced Chicken and Rice

This is the signature dish of Kurdistan, found at all major events and eaten in large quantities. Versions of Bryani are found throughout the Middle East and Central Asia. For instance, in Afghanistan it's called Qabuli Pilau and made with lamb (see page 58). Bryani Spice is available at Middle Eastern food markets.

1 **fryer chicken, fat and skin removed, quartered**

3 **quarts water**

3 **tablespoons salt**

1 **pound potatoes (2 cups), peeled and cubed**

1 **cup extra virgin olive oil**

4 **ounces raisins (½ cup)**

2 **ounces almond spears (¾ cup)**

½ **pound cut wheat vermicelli**

½ **teaspoon black pepper**

2 **tablespoons Bryani Spice**

4 **cups uncooked rice**

Boil the chicken in the water with 2 tablespoons of salt in a 6-quart saucepot for 45 minutes. Remove the chicken and reserve the broth.

Fry the potatoes in the olive oil in a 12-inch skillet on medium to medium-high heat until golden brown, turning occasionally. Remove and drain.

Fry the raisins in the same oil for a few seconds until plump. Remove and drain. Fry the almonds until golden brown. Remove and drain. Fry the vermicelli until light brown. Remove and drain.

Fry the chicken in remaining oil until golden brown, turning occasionally. Drain and allow to cool. Remove the chicken from the bones and shred.

Mix the chicken, potatoes, raisins, almonds and vermicelli with remaining salt, oil, black pepper, Bryani Spice and rice and two quarts of chicken broth in a 6-quart saucepot.

Simmer, covered, 20 minutes or until the rice is cooked, stirring occasionally.

Serves 6 to 8.

IPRACH
SEE RECIPE NEXT PAGE

Iprach
Stuffed Vegetables
(SEE PHOTOGRAPH PREVIOUS PAGE)

Known as Dolma throughout the Middle East, this dish is a mound of stuffed vegetables and grape leaves with chicken forming the foundation. This is a favorite of Suad's family. So much so, that on the snowy February afternoon she showed us how to make it, her sister-in-law showed up with two empty plates. The key to this dish is packing the chicken and stuffed ingredients tightly and then "pressure cooking" them with a weighted plate. Seven Spices and grape leaves are available at Middle Eastern food markets.

2 **Roma tomatoes**

2 **baby eggplants**

1 **green pepper**

4 **medium sweet yellow onions, peeled**

1 **pound round steak, chopped**

3 **garlic cloves, minced**

½ **cup extra virgin oil**

1 **6-ounce can tomato paste**

1 **6-ounce can tomato sauce**

½ **teaspoon black pepper**

¼ **teaspoon curry powder**

½ **tablespoon Seven Spices**

2 **tablespoons salt**

½ **tablespoon citric acid, or 2 tablespoons lemon juice (about 1 lemon)**

2 **cups uncooked rice**

1 **fryer chicken, quartered**

1 **small jar 4x6-inch grape leaves (also known as "vine leaves")**

Hollow out the tomatoes. Cut the eggplants in half widthwise and hollow out the insides. Chop the tops off the onions and green peppers and hollow them out, reserving the tops for later. On all the vegetables, be sure to leave ⅛- to ¼-inch walls. Set the hollowed out vegetables aside.

Chop the cores and fry with the steak and garlic in the olive oil in a 6-quart saucepot until the steak is browned.

Add the tomato paste, tomato sauce, black pepper, curry, Seven Spices, 1½ tablespoons salt, citric acid and uncooked rice to the saucepot and mix thoroughly.

Sprinkle the chicken with salt and place in the bottom of an 8-quart saucepot. Stuff cored vegetables with steak mixture. Replace their tops.

Use the remaining filling to stuff the grape leaves.

To stuff, separate one leaf from the jar. Lay on a flat surface. Place 2 tablespoons of rice mixture along one edge of leaf, leaving about 1½ inches on the right and left edges. Flip these edges over rice and roll into a "burrito" about 3 inches by 1 inch. Tightly pack the stuffed vegetables and grape leaves on top of the chicken.

Place saucepot on stove top. Add enough water to just barely reach the top of the stuffed vegetables, about 3 to 4 cups. Cover the contents with a ceramic plate just big enough to fit inside the pot. Place a ceramic mug filled with water on top to weigh down the plate and boil on medium-high heat until the water is almost gone, about 1 hour. Remove the plate, cover and cook on low for 45 minutes to 1 hour. If you smell the chicken burning, the dish is done.

Place a platter upside-down on top of saucepot and quickly flip contents onto platter. Slowly remove saucepot. The contents should form a tower of chicken, stuffed grape leaves and vegetables.

Serves 6 to 8

LAOS

Wedged between Vietnam and Thailand, Laos was bombed heavily by U.S. forces targeting North Vietnamese supply routes during the Vietnam War. So heavily that the country is known as the most bombed country in the history of modern warfare. But that is not why the refugees fled. Following the war, the country was taken over by the Pathet Lao, a political party with close ties to Vietnamese communists. Soon after, the Pathet Lao began rounding up anyone with even tacit relations to the former government or to U.S. forces. Word quickly spread that sentences in hard labor "re-education" camps would last 30 days or 30 years. Refugees began streaming out of Laos, first to Thailand and then to the United States. Manivanh and her family were among the 300,000—a tenth of the country's population—to flee. The family's crime: Manivanh's husband, a taxi driver, had accepted a few American fares.

"Your own gift you can present every moment with the cumulative force of a whole life's cultivation."

RALPH WALDO EMERSON,
SELF-RELIANCE

The black and white photograph doesn't seem to fit.

The young woman, her hair pulled back, is barely recognizable. Her smile is hard. Her eyes show fear. Her arms are crossed. Something happened to the woman in the photograph. The woman in the photograph is afraid.

The woman standing before me, holding the photograph, clearly isn't.

The woman before me wears designer eyeglasses, pressed slacks and a silk shirt. Her hair is fashionably trimmed. There is no fear in this place, a wood-paneled tailor shop in a nondescript strip mall on the suburban edge of this Midwest town. Her words are well-chosen. Words like *honey* and phrases like *you know what I'm sayin'* and *I just like to pick on her.*

They are not the words of a fearful person. Clearly, the fear is gone.

Manivanh Ratdavong, Lao refugee, survivor of the wars and camps in

Southeast Asia, has banished fear from this place. She swept it out and stitched herself a new life. A Made-in-America life, carefully sewn from the self-reliance of Emerson, the hard work and a strong belief in the God of the nation's Puritan forefathers, the organization of Henry Ford and JFK's *ask what you can do.*

◆　　　◆　　　◆

Self-reliance. *I had one interest when I arrived,* she says. *I wanted to be independent. I've wanted to be independent all my life.*

Manivanh and her husband, Kamphone, who works the nightshift for General Motors Corp., built their tailor shop from the family's living room to a thriving store with referrals from major retailers. *When I first came to the U.S. I just cried and cried,* she says between customers. Her delivery is matter of fact. This is a memory, not a nightmare.

I saw these beautiful jobs, these beautiful houses, and people would tell me that one day I would have that. I didn't believe them.

Her husband and four children had a new house built in the suburbs last year. Business is booming at the shop. Manivanh knows every customer. *I'm sweet,* she says. *I always call my customers "honey." Stuff like that. Of course, if they don't like my work, it doesn't matter. But that's how I am. Sweet.*

◆　　　◆　　　◆

Hard work. Manivanh never stops stitching or filing or tending to customers the entire time I spend with her. Her energy is boundless.

The door chimes. *Just a minute, honey.*

She rushes to the front. She says to one client, her diction slurred by a pin in her mouth: *You need to bring this one up a little bit.* To another: *You have a beautiful wife. No really, you are beautiful.*

In between, she continues our interview though I ask no questions. *Me and my husband have been married for 32 years. He never said "ugly." He always said "beautiful." We were an arranged marriage. I fell in love with him. I tell him, "You're lucky."*

She swoops into the backroom to speak to her husband in Lao. They laugh and she is back out front again.

◆　　　◆　　　◆

Spirituality. Raised a Buddhist, Manivanh and her family became Christian after coming to America. She says it was a simple progression begun by a miracle.

One day, not long after I arrived, I was sitting in my apartment. I was very lonely and I thought about this American woman I had met in the camp.

She spoke a little Lao and we really liked each other. So I prayed.

I prayed to God. To this God, I said "I don't know about you. But would you please send my friend to me?" I said "God, I really miss her. She's really nice. Show me a miracle. Show me that you have that power."

Minutes later, the woman knocked on the door. Her parents lived one town over.

◆　　　◆　　　◆

Organization. Every item in the shop has its place. Zippers and material line the walls by length, strength and color. The sewing machines are well oiled and conditioned. This is an assembly line. Each pincushion has a square piece of paper with an English word neatly written across. Manivanh picks one up. She studies English every day.

Ambition, she reads. *What does ambition mean?*

I tell her that it is the desire for success.

So it's like strength, energy.

Sometimes, I say. Sometimes it's not a good thing if someone has too much ambition. She frowns.

I don't think she believes me.

◆　　　◆　　　◆

Giving back. Last year Manivanh went back to Laos for the second time. As budget travelers returned to the country for statues and beer, she and her family went back to dig a well, build a bridge and give out school supplies paid for by the family and donations from her church. At her home, I watch the trip on video. The image is jumpy. Rain is pounding through thick jungle plants. I see clips of the electric well. I see the bridge before and after. I see children lining up for school supplies. They give curt bows as the family passes out supplies. In the middle of it, Manivanh tells me something quintessentially American.

We work hard for that money, she says. *I don't always get to see my husband. We are always tired, working as hard as we do. And I tell them in Laos "I don't want you just eating with that money. I want to know what you want for a career. What are you going to do to take care of yourself? How will you become strong women? How can I help you with that?"*

On the screen, Manivanh is smiling. She is playing the guitar. People are clapping and laughing and singing.

And the fear is gone.

She has found America.

She has found freedom.

The Ratdavongs brought this traditional doll back from Laos last year. She holds a sticky rice warmer in her hands.

Lao
Culture & Cuisine

All food in Laos starts with rice. Sticky rice, as the balls of thick-grained, steamed rice are known, is the principle crop in Laos and the basis for every meal. The rice is steamed and kept warm in intricately woven baskets. Children take a ball with them to munch on at school. Farmers take a ball for breaks from tending rice patties.

During meals, sticky rice is rolled into a ball in your left hand. You use your right hand to break off flattened hunks of rice and scoop the various meats, stir-fries and salads laid out and shared communally.

Food in Laos is very fresh, its people eat rare or nearly-rare meats and vegetables seasoned with fresh cilantro, lemon and hot Thai peppers. They use fermented sauces such as fish, soy and oyster sauces as seasonings, and sugar as a sweetener. The combinations vary markedly, based on ethnicity, region and even families.

Lao food is influenced by the frequent invasions the land-locked nation has seen during its history. Vietnam and Thailand have taken control many times and their influence extends to the food. As does the cuisine of the French, who controlled Laos in the 20th century.

At the same time, Laos is made up of various ethnic groups such as the Hmong and Mien hill tribes, which hold a different world view from the more Thai-oriented Ethnic Lao found in the cities.

Moreover, every Lao has her own way of cooking. Take Manivanh, for instance, she characterizes her cooking as a more modern take on Lao food, with French, Thai and Chinese influences included in her cuisine. *You can eat the food of 10 different Laos and all the food tastes different,* Manivanh says.

Meals are usually laid out on the floor or on low tables, with intricate cloths protecting the food from the ground. Men always eat first. But in Manivanh's home, everyone eats together. *In Laos, they say men sit down and the woman in the kitchen,* says Manivanh. *I say, no. I've got a good husband. He never complains about my food.*

Kang Jeud
Chicken Dumpling Soup

Manivanh makes this mild but tasty soup while she cooks other courses. The soup is simple to make and requires very little attention as it simmers. To rehydrate the mung bean noodles, place in hot water for 30 minutes.

1 small chicken breast with ribs

1½ quarts water

5 ounces sweet yellow onions (⅓ cup), finely minced

1 bunch green onions

¼ teaspoon black pepper

½ teaspoon salt

1 ounce mung bean noodles, rehydrated, cut into 1-inch lengths

½ tablespoon fish sauce

Cut the bones from the chicken breast with a sharp knife. Bring the water to a boil in a 4-quart saucepot. Add the chicken bones, reduce heat to simmer for 30 minutes. Skim the fat from the water as it surfaces.

In a food processor, finely mince the chicken breast, yellow and green onions, reserving ½ of the green tips. Mix in the black pepper and salt.

Increase heat to medium. Form teaspoon-sized dumplings from the minced chicken mixture and drop them into the simmering water. Simmer for 30 minutes. Skim the fat from the water as it surfaces.

Reduce heat to low and cook for 1 hour.

Add the remaining green onion tips, chopped into 1-inch lengths, and cook for 10 minutes.

Remove the chicken bones and discard. Add the noodles and fish sauce.

Add additional water if necessary. Serve immediately.

Serve 4 to 6

Khoua Phuk
Broccoli, Carrot and Chicken Stir-fry

M anivanh is a fastidious butcher. She says the key to any stir-fry is using the best cuts of meat and not overcooking the vegetables.

⅓ **large carrot, sliced**

1 **bunch broccoli**

⅓ **bunch green onions**

4 **tablespoons water**

1 **tablespoon flour**

1 **whole chicken breast, boned, skinned, cut into ¼-inch slices**

1 **clove garlic**

2 **tablespoons corn oil**

1 **tablespoon oyster sauce**

1 **tablespoon water**

⅔ **tablespoon sugar**

½ **tablespoon sesame oil**

1 **tablespoon soy sauce**

1 **teaspoon salt**

Cut the broccoli into individual florets. Cut the florets in half. Peel the stems and cut into 2-inch spears. Cut half the green onions into 2-inch spears. Chop the other half and set aside.

Blanche the carrot, broccoli and green onion spears in 2 quarts boiling water for 2 minutes. Drain and set aside.

Mix 1 tablespoon water and ⅓ tablespoon flour in a small bowl. Set aside.

Mix the chicken, 1 tablespoon water and remaining flour in a large bowl. Set aside.

Fry the garlic in corn oil in a wok on high heat until the garlic begins to brown. Add the chicken mixture, oyster sauce, chopped green onion, remaining water, sugar, sesame oil and soy sauce and fry until the chicken is 90 percent cooked.

Add the vegetables, flour and water mixture, and salt. Continue frying for about 20 more seconds, mixing well.

Remove from heat. Serve with rice.

Serves 6 to 8

Nho Jeun
Chicken Egg Rolls

(See photo next page)

These egg rolls exemplify Manivanh's modern Lao style. When she lived in Vientiane, few actually made egg rolls—a cuisine of China. Today, egg rolls with a tangy Ethnic Lao twist are the star of cooking among the diaspora. Gatherings feature mounds of these deep-fried delicacies. You can make them with beef, pork, chicken or all three. Check any Asian food market for mung bean vermicelli, oyster sauce and spring roll wrappers. To rehydrate the mung bean noodles, soak in hot water for 30 minutes.

2 **whole chicken breasts, boned and skinned**

½ **pound sweet yellow onions**

4½ **pounds green cabbage (4½ cups), thinly shredded and chopped**

1 **ounce dried mung bean vermicelli, rehydrated and chopped**

1 **medium carrot, shredded**

¾ **teaspoon pepper**

1 **teaspoon salt**

1 **tablespoon oyster sauce**

2 **eggs**

1 **pack 25 Chinese spring roll wrappers, thawed and separated**

corn oil for deep frying

Mince the chicken and onions in a food processor. Knead the cabbage, vermicelli, carrot, chicken, onions, pepper, salt, oyster sauce and one egg in a large bowl, making sure the ingredients are well-mixed and the minced chicken is broken apart.

Heat 3 inches of oil in a 6-quart saucepot over medium-high heat or to at least 400°F in a deep fryer. Separate the egg white from the last egg and set aside in a small bowl. Discard the yolk.

To roll, place 2 heaping tablespoons of the filling in a corner of the wrapper about 1 inch from the corner and the edges. Dab egg white on the far corner. Fold the lower corner over the line of filling. Roll tightly until ½ the wrapper is rolled. Fold in the left and right corners and continue to roll tightly until the upper corner is reached. The egg white will keep the egg roll stuck together. Roll 8 egg rolls. Place together in the deep fryer. Fry until the ends of the egg rolls darken, about 10 minutes. Remove and drain. Continue with the rest of the filling and wrappers.

Makes 25 egg rolls

CHICKEN EGG ROLLS
SEE RECIPE PREVIOUS PAGE

Laab
Beef Salad

This is the quintessential Ethnic Lao dish, a traditional main course eaten with a handful of sticky rice and fresh wedges of lettuce and cucumber. Laab has the liveliness of cilantro, heat of hot peppers, the sweet and sour of Thai fish sauce, and the richness of lean chopped beef. It's served cold. Of all the dishes Manivanh makes at home, Laab—often made with chicken as laab kai—is the one that everyone asks for. Fish sauce and Thai red peppers are available from Asian food markets. If you only try one Lao dish in your life, this is the one.

1½ **pounds sirloin roast, coarsely chopped**

2 **teaspoons lime juice (about ¼ lime)**

½ **bunch of cilantro (1 cup), coarsely chopped**

½ **tablespoon salt**

½ **tablespoon sugar**

1 **tablespoon Thai fish sauce**

½ **teaspoon ground red pepper**

2 **bunches green onions, minced**

5 **Thai red chiles, chopped**

lettuce wedges (optional)

cucumber slices (optional)

Brown the beef to medium-rare in a large, non-stick wok on high heat, stirring often. Transfer to a large bowl. Add the lime juice, cilantro, salt, sugar and fish sauce. Mix by hand, being sure to break up any chunks of beef.

Add the ground red pepper, green onions and Thai red chiles and stir with a spoon.

Serve with lettuce wedges, cucumber slices and rice.

Serves 4 to 6

EPILOGUE

KOSOVO

Remzija had a baby two weeks after we met and named him Bikem Ademi. He's a robust, crawling 8-month-old. Remzija is spending the summer taking her children to a new beach by her apartment while her husband, Rabit, works at night. Money is a bit tight right now, she says through a translator, but maybe next year they will visit Kosovo.

SOMALIA

Isha's children and grandchildren continue to grow. Isha does all she can to spend as much time as possible with them. We visited one recent Saturday. While others put in overtime at the factory where she is an inspector, Isha was at home with her children and grandchildren. *I don't work overtime,* Isha said. *My time is for my family.*

SUDAN

Sara joined the Sudanese Women's Society in Washington, D.C., her daughter Tahani reports. *She goes to all the meetings and events. There are many young women in the group. They all look up to her.* Sara's daughter Noon attends Howard University while Zina waits to hear from George Mason University. Tahani, a medical doctor in Sudan, studies for board examinations to become a doctor in the U.S. Sara's son Mohamed, still just 14, has grown taller than 6 feet. *There are a lot of girls interested in him,* said Tahani. *But he just laughs and says, "Mom says no girls!"*

CUBA

Zohiris will start a nursing program at a local community college in the fall, her husband Leonel reports. During Zohiris' preparatory studies at the college she was named to the Dean's List three times. Meanwhile, Zohiris works at a local hotel and cares for her children. The couple's daughter Leiris is entering the sixth grade while their son Leonel Jr. will start elementary school. Leonel Sr. is now a cashier at the local bakery and is working on a novel. *It's about life and war and love and peace,* he said. *It's about everything.*

AFGHANISTAN

Wasima watches the mailbox closely these days. Early in the summer of 2003, Wasima learned that she could get state income to compensate her helping her father. She filled out the paperwork and has been watching the mailbox for the first check every day. She's also waiting for her official registration papers to arrive from a local community college. She will start academic English classes this fall. Early in the spring she filed a Red Cross Trace in the search for her missing sister. To date, there has been no response.

COLOMBIA

Clara is stretching into her new American life. She purchased a nearly new Toyota Echo in the summer of 2003 and moved into an apartment located closer to her work. She was saddened by the death of Mimi from pneumonia early this summer. She wrote us an e-mail that read in part: *I gave her the best in her last days. I told her, "I love you Mimi." And she said, "I love you, too, honey. What will I do without you?" I know she is in Heaven now and I know she will be another angel in my life.*

KURDISTAN

Suad, Hassan and Zana moved to Indianapolis, Ind., in March 2003. On its face, it was a random move. But it suited the family well. *We get bored sometimes,* Suad explains. *So we move to another place.* Suad finds Indianapolis *so beautiful.* But she continues to miss her family back in Iraq. *It's so lonely here,* she said. The pizzeria where Hassan works as a deliverer was robbed at gunpoint recently. The gunman took the wallets of all the employees. They gave Hassan's back because it contained no money.

LAOS

In April, Manivanh's daughter, Phonethipphavanh married Vilasack Phothisane, a member of the Lao community from Holland, Michigan. She said the wedding at a downtown hotel in Grand Rapids was beautiful. Now she's relaxing a bit. But not too much. *God never leaves his space,* she says. *That means I still have work to do. I think God is calling me to serve him by doing action. I had a feeling not too long ago that I'll be going back to Laos, to bring the Good News, next year. At the same time, I will do what God plans.*

INDEX

the Global Workshop, LLC

The Global Workshop educates communities on their own diversity using traditional and new media. We create practical tools for practical solutions in cultural diversity, the environment, aid and economic development, poverty and migration. Our mission is to generate community response to these global issues by producing marketable CDs, books, web sites, traveling exhibits, and presentations. We believe in in-depth storytelling. We value the space and creativity new media allow. We focus on content and foster change.

VINCENT DELGADO

A partner with The Global Workshop, LLC, and coordinator of the Refugee Development Center and Refugee Services public outreach, Vincent Delgado has a decade of experience speaking and writing about international and refugee issues. The award-winning newspaper and magazine journalist can be found eating copious quantities of Iprach and Laab in Lansing, Michigan.

JEREMY HERLICZEK

Jeremy Herliczek, a partner with The Global Workshop, LLC, is a photographer and educator who has traveled worldwide covering environmental issues, disability and cultural colonialism. Currently staff photographer for NOISE, a magazine in Lansing, his work has appeared in major newspapers and magazines. He refuses to admit any guilt regarding "the onion incident" in our test kitchen, and after countless hours designing this book, he looks forward to getting away from a desk and into a river kayak.

BECKY SHINK

Becky Shink is a partner with The Global Workshop, LLC, and an award-winning photojournalist with expertise in environmental and community education. She has traveled extensively throughout Central America and the Caribbean. Her work has appeared in major newspapers and magazines. She is still wondering what to do with the onions and garlic stuck to her kitchen ceiling following a blending mishap while cooking Bolawnee.

A TASTE OF
FREEDOM
A CULINARY JOURNEY WITH
AMERICA'S REFUGEES

ORDER FORM

___ book(s) at $14.99 each: _____
Tax (0.6%): _____
S&H: _____
Total: _____

Shipping & Handling
1st copy $2.50
Each additional copy $0.75

Please allow up to
14 days for delivery.

Ship Books To:
(Please print clearly)

Name _____
Address _____
City _____State_____Zip_____
Telephone (___)_____
E-mail _____
Organization _____

Mail this form and a check or money order to:

The Global Workshop, LLC
P.O. Box 11126
Lansing, MI 48901

For questions or comments please e-mail us at
GlobalWorkshop@hotmail.com

Advance praise for *A Taste of Freedom*:

"Rich in detail and written with passion, *A Taste of Freedom* is an eye opening chronicle of the plight of refugees in America. They came to this country with nothing save the culinary traditions and recipes of their homelands. A gastronomic gold mine. Bravo!"

Chef Eric Villegas,
Owner of Restaurant Villegas &
star of the cooking show
"A Fork in the Road."

"The spaghetti, hot dogs and tacos that yesterday's refugees and immigrants introduced us to are today's quintessentially American foods. Refugees coming to America now continue to enrich our culture not only with their Kabobs and Arepas, Sambusas and Black Beans, but with their love of freedom and their zest for the American Dream. *A Taste of Freedom* offers intimate portraits of some of these courageous individuals, the persecution that led them here, and their struggles to build new lives."

Lavinia Limon,
Executive Director of the U.S.
Committee for Refugees (USCR)

"What better way for us to learn about the plight of refugees than by reading a beautiful book detailing their stories, their traditions and their foods. In *A Taste of Freedom*, we learn about refugees and the importance of preserving their heartfelt stories for future generations. The words are captivating and, like any good book, it is difficult to put down. It is truly inspirational and helps to give a voice to refugees."

Elissa Goldman,
Libraries for the Future